Paul Tapsell is a barrister and mediator who has been based in Becket Chambers, Canterbury since 1993. His practice encompasses a wide range of civil work, including Condemnation and Restoration proceeding, and he regularly appears in a Courts and Tribunals in cases involving the seizure of goods, vehicles and/or cash, acting for individuals or public authorities.

A Practical Guide to Challenging Seizures under the Customs and Excise Management Act 1979

A Practical Guide to Challenging Seizures under the Customs and Excise Management Act 1979

Paul Tapsell

Barrister, Middle Temple

LLB

Law Brief Publishing

Published 2024 by Law Brief Publishing, an imprint of Law Brief Publishing Ltd
30 The Parks
Minehead
Somerset
TA24 8BT

www.lawbriefpublishing.com

Paperback: 978-1-916698-39-0

PREFACE

Condemnation and Restoration proceedings are something of a niche area of law, and this book is intended to provide a single point of reference for practitioners (and individuals) dealing with the aftermath of the seizure of goods and/or vehicles by Border Force under powers from the Customs and Excise Management Act 1979.

The post-Brexit replacement of the concept of "personal use" with the return of "travellers' allowances" in respect of excise goods and the 2022 Supreme Court decision in Flynn Pharma have provided a convenient opportunity to review and analyse the relevant issues and processes when challenging (or defending) such seizures.

The law is stated as at the 1st June 2024.

Paul Tapsell
Becket Chambers
Canterbury
June 2024

CONTENTS

TABLE OF AUTHORITIES

INTRODUCTION

The legislation relating to the condemnation of goods under, principally the Customs and Excise Management Act 1979 ("CEMA" or "the Act") involves a number of technical terms (many of which are not formally defined in the legislation) so, for the avoidance of doubt, in summary:

"Appellant" in restoration proceedings in the First Tier Tribunal Tax Chamber is the individual (or company) challenging a Review Decision by a Border Force Officer dealing with a request to restore seized goods.

"Border Force" refers to the authority responsible for customs controls at airports and ports in the UK (although they have powers beyond the physical extent of those places). Previous case law refers to earlier incarnations of the equivalent bodies.

"CEMA" is the Customs and Excise Management Act 1979; unless indicated otherwise all references to sections relate to CEMA and all references to paragraph numbers are to Schedule 3 of CEMA.

"Claim/Claimant" refers in Condemnation Proceedings to the individual who seeks the return of goods seized pursuant to the powers under CEMA (usually Border Force or, in the legislation and case law, the Commissioners for Customs and Excise or the Director of Border Revenue)

"Complainant"	in Condemnation Proceedings relates to the authority (Border Force) bringing the proceedings ("Complaint") for the condemnation of goods, etc. seized under CEMA.
"Condemnation"	relates to the proceedings, usually in the Magistrates Court but occasionally in the High Court or, on appeal from the Magistrates' Court, in the Crown Court, where an individual challenges the lawfulness of the seizure of their property and the Court determines whether the goods were "liable to forfeiture" and, if so, "Condemns" them or, if not, orders their return to the Claimant.
"Detention"	relates to the initial retention of items by, for present purposes, officers Border Force, for example while inquiries are being pursued.
"Forfeiture"	relates to the process whereby an individual is permanently deprived of items.
"Review"	relates to an internal process under section 152(b) CEMA within Border Force where an individual challenges a Border Force officer's decision not to return items seized (usually upon payment of a fee, often equivalent to the value and/or duty payable on the seized items plus a penalty element).
"Respondent"	in restoration proceedings in the First Tier Tribunal Tax Chamber refers to the seizing authority (i.e. Border Force).

"Restoration"	relates to a challenge of a Review decisions by the individual making an application to the First Tier Tribunal (Tax Chamber) ("the Tribunal").
"Seizure"	relates to the process following a decision by Border Force to retain the items, which decision is then subject to challenge by the individuals affected.

PART ONE

SEIZURE

CHAPTER ONE

FORFEITURE: THE STATUTORY FRAMEWORK

"Liable to Forfeiture"

The Customs and Excise Management Act 1979 ("CEMA" or "the Act") makes numerous references to items being seized and/or detained as being "liable to forfeiture" in a wide range of circumstances but fails to provide any statutory definition of the phrase.

Section 49 CEMA provides the principal provision relating to liability to forfeiture:

> "49(1) Where -
>
> (a) …any imported goods, being goods chargeable on their importation with customs or excise duty, are, without payment of that duty, (i) unshipped in any port, (ii) unloaded from any aircraft in the United Kingdom …
>
> (b) any goods are imported, landed or unloaded contrary to any prohibition or restriction for the time being in force with respect thereto under or by virtue of any enactment; or
>
> (c) any goods, being goods chargeable with any duty or goods the importation of which is for the time being prohibited or restricted by or under any enactment, are found, whether before or after the unloading thereof, to

> have been concealed in any manner on board any ship or aircraft or, while in Northern Ireland, in any vehicle; or
>
> "(d) any goods are imported or concealed in a container holding goods of a different description; or
>
> (e) any imported goods are found, whether before or after delivery, not to correspond with the entry made thereof; or
>
> (f) any imported goods are concealed or packed in a manner appearing to be intended to deceive and officers,
>
> those goods shall, subject to subsection (2) below, be liable to forfeiture."

Further legislation deals with the imposition of duty on goods (see Chapter 3 "**Excise Goods and Personal Allowances**" below) and prohibition or restrictions (e.g. in respect of weapons, drugs, indecent or obscene material, etc.).

Similarly, section 78(4) provides that any goods subject to duty which are not declared or are concealed are liable to forfeiture and other provisions create such liability, for instance, where a ship, aircraft or a vehicle has been "constructed, adapted, altered or fitted in any manner for the purpose of concealing goods" (section 88)

The Act grants extensive powers of search, seizure and detention to Border Force (or other persons acting on their behalf) and provides that:

> "139(1) Any thing liable to forfeiture under the customs and excise Acts may be seized or detained by any officer or constable or any member of Her Majesty's armed forces or coastguard."

The lack of any statutory definition of "liable to forfeiture" gave rise to questions regarding the lawfulness of the detention of goods which were subsequently found not to be liable to forfeiture (for example following further inquiries) and was finally resolved in the Supreme Court in (**R (Eastenders Cash & Carry plc & Others) v Revenue and Customs Commissioners** [2014] UKSC 34, where it was decided:

> " ... the detention of the goods was lawful because there had been no abuse of authority on the part of the officers; and there had been no such abuse because their authority to examine the goods in order to determine the duty payable, or (by implication) whether the goods were liable to forfeiture, carried with it, by necessary implication, an authority to detain the goods for such time as was reasonably necessary in order to make that determination. Where the determination required the making of inquiries, going beyond an inspection of the goods themselves, it was lawful to detain the goods for such time as was reasonably necessary to make those inquiries" (paragraph 35).

Section 139(1A), brought in as a response to the **Eastenders** litigation expressly allows the detention of items where the detaining officer "reasonably suspects" that the items may be liable to forfeiture.

Section 141 goes on to make provision for the forfeiture of ships, vehicles, etc. used in connection with goods liable to forfeiture ("Secondary Forfeiture"):

> "141(1) Without prejudice to any other provision of the Customs and Excise Management Acts 1979, where any thing has become liable to forfeiture under the customs and excise Acts-

> (a) any ship, aircraft, vehicle, animal, container (including any article of passengers' baggage) or any other thing whatsoever which has been used for the carriage, handling, deposit or concealment of the thing so liable to forfeiture, either at a time when it was so liable or for the purposes of the commission of the offence for which it later became so liable; and
>
> (b) any other thing mixed, packed or found with the thing so liable
>
> shall also be liable to forfeiture."

and section 141(2) goes on to render any "tackle, apparel or furniture" of any "ship, aircraft, vehicle or animal" also liable to forfeiture.

Section 144 CEMA (see below) provides immunity for the Commissioners in respect of any losses incurred by an individual if there were reasonable grounds for the original seizure, regardless of the subsequent decision that the item was not, in fact, liable to forfeiture and so the item was not condemned.

Schedule 2A of the Act makes provisions for the procedure where items have been detained which includes allowing detention for up to 30 days (whereupon it is deemed to be seized, para 2(3)) and requiring the Commissioners (i.e. Border Force) to:

> "take reasonable steps to give written notice of the detention of any thing, and of the grounds for the detention, to any person who to their knowledge was, at the time of the detention, the owner or one of the owners of the things" (para 3(1)).

Written notice is not required where the detention takes place in the presence of the owner of the thing, their servant or agent, "a person who has (or appears to have) possession or control of the thing being detained" (para 3(2(ba)), the master or commander of a ship or aircraft, or a vehicle operator (where the goods are detained from a vehicle).

Schedule 3 of CEMA sets out the provisions relating to forfeiture and condemnation proceedings and is dealt with in detail in Part 3 below.

Historically, the majority of contested condemnation cases involved situations where individuals came into the country with excess excise goods (i.e. alcohol or tobacco) and the goods were seized under section 49(1) as being not for personal use and the vehicle being used to transport the goods was often seized by Border Force under section 141.

This gave rise to situations where, for example, the owner of a car which was being driven by their partner to take a group of friends to the continent, had their car seized because one of the passengers had excise goods over the limit. In such a case (**Customs and Excise Commissioners v Newbury** [2003] 1 WLR 2131) it was established that a Court considering condemnation proceedings had to take into account to proportionality of condemning the car seized as being liable to forfeiture pursuant to section 141 (see Chapter 9, Proportionality, below).

Since Brexit the "personal use" provisions under the Excise Goods (Holding, Movement and Duty Point) Regulations 2010 (with, under Regulation 13(4), "minimum indicative guidelines" including 90 litres of wine(including a maximum of 60 litres of sparkling wine), 10 litres of spirits, 110 litres of beer and 800 cigarettes or 1 kg of tobacco) were removed and replaced by the reintroduction of significantly reduced "Personal Allowances" for travellers (e.g. 18 litres of wine, 4 litres of spirits, 42 litres of beer, and 200 cigarettes or 250g of tobacco). This has significantly reduced the economic attraction of the "booze cruise" or "tobacco run" for individuals but increased the risk of the unwary traveller having their vehicle seized.

Similarly, an individual failing to declare (non-excise) goods purchased abroad worth over £390 (or £270 if they arrived by private plane or boat) or a person driving a vehicle which had been adapted by a previous owner for the purposes of concealing goods (regardless of whether any such concealed goods were present or the new owner was aware of the adaptation) is liable to have those goods or that vehicle seized by Border Force.

CHAPTER TWO

CHALLENGING THE SEIZURE

Condemnation or Restoration?

Once items have been seized (whether upon interception or after a period of detention), CEMA section 139(6) provides that:

> "Schedule 3 to this Act shall have effect for the purposes of forfeitures, and of proceedings for the condemnation of any thing as being forfeited, under the customs and excise Acts."

Condemnation proceedings, where an individual disputed that the "thing" or things are liable to forfeiture and so challenges the legality of the seizure, usually in the Magistrates' Court, are considered in Part 3 below.

Alternatively (or as well as pursing condemnation proceedings) it is open to an individual to seek a review of the decision to seize the item(s) and to request that Border Force exercise its powers under section 152(b) of the Act to

> "restore subject to such conditions (if any) as they think proper, any thing forfeited or seized under [the customs and excise] Acts"

and, if the individual is dissatisfied with the review decision, they can challenge that decision in the First Tier Tribunal, Tax Chamber. This process starts from the position that the seizure was lawful but the decision thereafter not to restore the item(s) seized was not reasonable. The Restoration process is considered in Part 4, below.

The twin-track approach inevitably causes issues and has been the subject of judicial criticism, most notably in **Gascoyne v Customs and Excise Commissioners** [2004] EWCA Civ 1162, where Lord Justices Buxton, Carnworth and Brooke, opined upon the fact that "the procedure has a number of elements which appear to have grown up over the years and which do not always easily fit with each other" (para 5), the "very unsatisfactory mismatch of the two statutory procedures (para 89) and the "unsatisfactory condition of the statutory provisions" (para 91), respectively. Sadly, Parliament has not found time to deal with these criticisms.

It is essential for any request to challenge the seizure to indicate clearly whether the individual wishes to pursue condemnation proceedings (as a Notice of Claim under Schedule 3 para 3) or by way of a Review seeking restoration of the seized items under section 152(b) or both. **Gascoyne** confirms that where an individual apparently seeks the return of his goods (rather than also clearly challenging their liability to forfeiture) it was reasonable for Customs to take the view that he simply sought a review under section 152(b).

A similar point was considered in **GLL BVK Internationaler Immobilien Spezialfonds v Revenue and Customs Commissioners** [2019] UKUT 17 (TCC) where the Tribunal upheld an officer's reasonable assessment of the intention of a letter of claim (in connection with income tax repayments) as opposed to a wider interpretation sought by the taxpayer.

PART TWO

GROUNDS FOR SEIZURE

CHAPTER THREE

EXCISE GOODS AND PERSONAL ALLOWANCES

Historically the majority of condemnation proceedings were brought as a result of individuals purchasing excise goods for their "personal use" and having the goods, and often the vehicle they were travelling in, seized.

Determination of whether goods were for "personal use" involved considering, for instance, the Excise Goods (Holding, Movement and Duty Point) Regulations 2010 (S.I. 2010 No. 593) which set out a number of factors to be taken into account when deciding whether goods were being brought into the UK for personal use (in which case duty was not payable) or for commercial purposes (in which case duty was payable and, pursuant to section 49 CEMA, the failure to declare the goods and to pay duty rendered the goods liable to forfeiture).

The factors included the quantity of the goods and, in particular, whether they were in excess of the "Guideline Quantities" or "Minimum Indicative Levels" (from Regulation 13(4)(h) reflecting the amounts prescribed by EU Council Directive 2008/118/EC), as well as the reasons for, circumstances and manner of the importation, the conduct of the individual and the financing of the purchase.

If the goods were found to be for personal use then they, and the vehicle, would be returned (or compensation paid if the goods had been destroyed) but if the goods were found not to have been for personal use then the proportionality of the forfeiture of the vehicle, if any, would be considered (**Customs and Excise Commissioners v Newbury** [2003] 1 WLR 2131 – see Chapter 9, Proportionality, below).

Post the Brexit-transition period (i.e. from 1st January 2021), the concept of personal use ceased to exist and there was a return to the regime of personal ("duty-free") allowances under the Travellers Allowances Order 1994 (SI 1994/955) as amended by the Travellers' Allowances and Miscellaneous Provisions (EU Exit) Regulations 2020 (SI 2020/1412) which increased the original allowances, although they are significantly lower than permitted under the personal use arrangements.

Separate rules exist for individuals travelling to or from Northern Ireland as a result of the Northern Ireland trade agreement (and, at the time of writing, may be subject to change) and are not covered here – guidance is available on the gov.uk website.

Excise Goods

The present (June 2024) allowances are:

Alcohol:

42 litres of beer and

18 litres of still wine and

4 litres of spirits or liquors over 22% alcohol or

9 litres of sparkling wine, fortified wines or other alcoholic drinks up to 22%

(the allowances for spirits, etc. and sparkling wine can be split, e.g. 2 litres of spirits and 4.5 litres of sparkling wine, i.e. one half of each allowance, is permitted)

Tobacco

200 cigarettes,

100 cigarillos or

50 cigars, 250g tobacco or 200 sticks of "heating tobacco"

(again, the tobacco allowance can be split across the various categories).

There are no personal allowances for individuals under 17 years of age and so any excise goods must be declared and duty paid. In theory such goods could be brought in (if legitimately purchased abroad given the individual's age) but the likelihood is that, (declared or not) if found, they would be seized as liable to forfeiture.

Personal Allowance – Other Goods

In addition, an individual is entitled to bring in other goods worth up to £390 (or £270 if the individual has arrived by private boat or plane) but if the items are worth more than the prescribed sums then import VAT and customs duty is payable on the whole value of the items (not just the amount over the threshold).

Given the modest level of the threshold (and the often ignored requirement to declare goods worth more than the prescribed sums when leaving the UK) and the relatively low threshold for detention and/or seizure (i.e. under section 139 of 139(1A) CEMA), where an individual has purchased goods worth more than £390 abroad but fails to declare them on their return to the UK or returns to the UK with an item which looks as if it may have been purchased while they were away (e.g. old jewellery they took out with them but which has been repaired, cleaned or worked on while they were away) there is a risk they will have that item seized.

Declaring Goods

If an individual goes over their allowance they must declare the goods; this can be done online up to 5 days before they arrive in the UK or before crossing the UK border (i.e. prior to passing the UK Border Controls, which may be in the departure terminal e.g. the UK Border controls at the "French" terminal of the Channel Tunnel) and must pay tax and duty on all the goods in the category where they have exceeded their allowance.

Goods made or produced in the EU

Where goods have been grown or made and purchased in the European Union (and are being brought in from a EU country) an individual can ,when declaring the goods, claim a zero rate of customs duty on those items; if the goods are worth less than £1,000 then the individual may be asked to provide evidence of the provenance of the goods e.g. a label or packaging confirming where it was produced or documentation from the producer confirming it was hand-made or grown in the EU (along with the invoice confirming the price paid or value of the items). Where the total value of the goods is in excess of £1,000 documentation may be required to confirm the identity of the seller, the items purchased and a "statement of origin" confirming that the item is made from materials from the EU and, if the total value of the goods is over £5,500, providing the seller's registered exporter number.

In the absence of satisfactory evidence that the zero rate of customs duty applies and/or in the event the Customs duty is not paid then the items become liable to forfeiture pursuant to section 49(1)(a) CEMA.

The online declaration service provides for the calculation of Import VAT and customs and excise duties as long as the individual remains within the "Upper Threshold" or limits on the amount of excise goods which can be declared.

These Upper Thresholds are set out in Schedule 2 to the 1994 Travellers' Allowances Order 1994 (inserted by the Travellers' Allowances … Regulations 2020) and reflect the Guideline Quantities under the 2010 Regulations, i.e.

110 litres of beer

90 litres of still wine

60 litres of sparkling wine

20 litres of cider

20 litres of sparkling cider not exceeding 5.5% ABV

20 litres of cider with ABV between 5.5% and 8.5% ABV

20 litres of other fermented products

10 litres of spirits

and, for tobacco products

800 cigarettes

1kilogram hand rolling tobacco

> 1 kilogram of other smoking tobacco and chewing tobacco
>
> 200 cigars
>
> 400 cigarillos (a cigar weighing no more than 3 grams each)
>
> 800 sticks of tobacco for heating

The Schedule provide details of the "simplified rate" of excise and customs duty payable in respect of each type of product although the specific rates of excise and customs duty are subject to regular amendment by Statutory Instruments or, following a budget, the relevant Finance Act.

By way of examples, pursuant to amendments to the duty rates under the Alcoholic Products (Excise Duty) Regulations 2023 (SI 2023/806) and Finance Act 2024 section 23(2)(a), as at June 2024 under the simplified regime:

> Beer attracts excise duty of £0.88 per litre (but no customs duty),
>
> Still Wine attracts excise duty of £3.28 per litre and customs duty of £0.26 per litre,
>
> Spirits are subject to excise duty of £11.88 per litre (but no customs duty) and
>
> Hand Rolling Tobacco attracts simplified excise duty of £412.32 per kilo and customs duty of 70% of the total value of the item.

In addition, Import VAT (at the current rate of 20%) may also be chargeable on any purchases over the personal allowance.

The economic advantages of the "booze cruise" where day trippers would go to France or Belgium to stock up on excise goods for their "personal use", which included bona fide gifts, but not circumstances involving

> "the transfer of the goods to another person for money or money's worth (including any reimbursement of expenses incurred in connection with obtaining them)" (Regulation 13(5)(b) of the Excise Goods ... Regulations 2010)

are, inevitably, reduced significantly as a result of the new regime.

Further provisions apply in respect of other goods (i.e. non-excise goods): for goods with a value of less than £630 the online system applies a flat rate of 2.5% for customs duty whereas if the total value of goods exceeds £630 then various rates between 0% and 16% apply to "other goods".

A failure to declare all goods correctly will render them liable to forfeiture pursuant to section 49 CEMA and, potentially, the vehicle, etc. used to transport them and or any things found mixed, packed, etc. with them (section 141(1) CEMA.)

CHAPTER FOUR

OTHER COMMON SITUATIONS

Vehicles adapted for smuggling

Section 88 CEMA provides that vehicles, etc. "constructed, adapted, altered or fitted in any manner for the purpose of concealing goods ...shall be liable to forfeiture"; this raises the possibility that an innocent purchaser of a vehicle which has been adapted (and potentially used) for smuggling by others and then sold on, often at auction where the purchaser may have had little or no opportunity to examine the vehicle closely, has their vehicle seized and subjected to condemnation proceedings.

As the vehicle, rather than the owner of the vehicle, is the subject of the proceedings the individual's state of mind or knowledge of the adaptation, etc. is irrelevant (see **Mudie**, **Goldsmith**, **Air Canada**, etc. at Chapter 6, Condemnation Proceedings, below) and, historically, the view has been taken that the effect of para 6 of Schedule 3 CEMA is that if there is, as a finding of fact, a concealment then it is mandatory for the vehicle to be condemned as forfeit.

This strict approach limited the individual's arguments in such a situation to whether there was, in fact, an adaptation or concealment as opposed to, for instance, a natural void in the fabric or structure of the vehicle but, in light of **Newbury** (and the context of the remainder of the judgment in in **Fox v Customs and Excise Commissioners** [2002] EWHC 1244 (Admin), referred to below), there is no reason why the principles of proportionality should not apply, albeit that there is inevitably a strong but, it is suggested, rebuttable presumption that there are good public policy reasons for (and therefore a public interest in) removing vehicles which have been adapted for smuggling from circulation.

The factors that might impact the proportionality of forfeiture may include:

the personal circumstances of the individual,

the circumstances of the purchase and use of the vehicle,

the value of the vehicle,

the likely cost (and any other implications) of the adaptation – it may be that cutting into the chassis of the vehicle to create the concealment has rendered it unroadworthy,

any legitimate personal adaptations made to the vehicle by the individual (although such works may suggest that the individual was, or should have been, aware of the adaptation),

how long the vehicle has been owned by the individual (and whether it has been worked on, maintained or MOT'd without the concealment being detected),

the conduct of the individual in the course of the interception and any subsequent correspondence and/or proceedings (e.g. a refusal to answer questions contrasted with a willingness to cooperate)

any previous dealings the individual has had with Border Force and any offers made to disable or remove the concealment.

Given that the Court's powers in condemnation proceedings are "all or nothing" (Hale J in **Newbury** at para [23], see Chapter 9, Proportionality, below), i.e. it has no power, for instance, to require the individual to remove the concealment or restore the vehicle's original structure as a condition for refusing to condemn the vehicle, the individual in such a situation should consider pursuing a review of the seizure under section 152(b) CEMA (and, if necessary, appeal the refusal to restore the vehicle in the First Tier Tribunal) as a back-up in the eventuality that the proportionality arguments fail to persuade the Court.

Foreign Purchases

As indicated above, the relatively modest value of "other goods" permitted under an individual's personal allowance (i.e. £390) creates the possibility that an individual who purchases a valuable item abroad (or has work done to, for instance, a piece of jewellery they took with them) may have that item seized on their return to the United Kingdom.

In theory an individual is required to declare any valuable items when they leave the UK although the reality is that this rarely happens, but an individual coming into the UK, if stopped, may well be expected to produce evidence of the provenance and value of items which have been, or appear to have been, purchased abroad and, if the items are, or appear to be, over the personal allowance and have not been declared they may be seized.

Red Diesel

Similar considerations will apply, for example in cases involving "red diesel": the use of "red diesel" (i.e. a heavy oil, often heating oil, not intended as a fuel for general vehicles and subject to a lower rate of duty and which is dyed red) in vehicles other than those expressly excepted and identified in Schedule 1A to the Hydrocarbon Oil Duties Act 1979 is prohibited and section 13(6) of that Act provides that any red diesel being used in or supplied to a road vehicle is liable to forfeiture.

Border Force and other officers are permitted to check and take samples of fuel being used by vehicles (and such checks may take place anywhere in the UK) and, in the event that red diesel is detected the oil is seized along with, usually, the vehicle.

Duty Suspension Movements

Commercial importers (or exporters) of excise goods have the facility moving excise goods in (or out) of the UK between bonded warehouses under "duty suspension" pursuant to the Excise Goods (Holding, Movement and Duty Point) Regulations 2010 (SI 2010 No. 593) and Regulation 88 renders goods moved in contravention of the Regulations liable to forfeiture. Any duty is payable when the goods are released from the receiving bonded warehouse and the movement is covered by a bond to secure the duty payable.

The scheme involves an electronic Administrative Document ("eAD") being created by the consignor (i.e. often a bonded warehouse dispatching the goods) prior to the goods being released, the eAD is logged onto the Excise Management and Control System ("EMCS") and, once validated a unique Administrative Reference Code ("ARC") is issued to both the consignor and the consignee (the bonded warehouse receiving the goods).

The eAD records the date and time of despatch and the arrival date (giving the document a limited life span depending on the estimated journey time) and the ARC documentation relating to that consignment must travel with the goods. The documentation for the load, including the CMR (Contrat de Transport International de Merchandises par Route), will also identify the details of the supplier, the end recipient of the goods and the transporter and, usually, the tractor and trailer units being used to transport the goods. Once received the consignee records receipt and logs the details of any excesses, shortages or losses i.e. any difference between the goods despatched and received onto the EMCS (and HMRC may investigate any apparent shortages or losses).

The system is intended to be secure and to ensure that each movement has a unique set of papers but it is open to abuse whereby "shadow" loads of excise goods, purporting to operate under a single ARC, are despatched to the UK with goods acquired "duty paid" in the foreign country. As long as a single load arrives at the official consignee bonded warehouse to ensure the load is logged as received on the EMCS the load will appear to have been in accordance with the procedure.

Where there is an interception and discrepancies are noted with the documentation or in respect of the load not matching the details held on the ECMS (e.g. there are different quantities of different excise goods) the load, and usually the tractor and trailer unit will be seized as liable to forfeiture under Regulation 88 and section 139 CEMA.

Investigation of such cases will often involve the production and examination of travel records of other vehicles where the same or similar vehicle registration or load/CMR details, or close matches, are being transported within the life of the ARC.

As indicated above, condemnation proceedings will involve an assessment of the proportionality of forfeiture given the circumstances of the case and in the light of the explanation given by the owner of the goods, and/or the vehicle as to the reasons for any discrepancy but from the starting point of the strong public interest and policy reasons for ensuring strict and robust controls of excise goods movements (given the financial impact of the loss of tax revenue in relation to such movements).

Suspected Excise Evasion

Criminal sanctions exist for persons "knowingly concerned in the taking of any steps with a view to the fraudulent evasion, whether by himself or another, of any duty of excise on any goods" (section 170B(1) CEMA).

Section 170B(2) provides that

> "Where any person is guilty of an offence under this section, the goods in respect of which the offence was committed shall be liable to forfeiture".

and in **Amber Services Europe Ltd v Director of Border Revenue** [2015] EWHC 3665 (Admin) it was argued that as there had not been a conviction in respect of the particular goods involved in that case (unprocessed tobacco leaf which was found to be intended for processing and sale without payment of excise duty) the goods were not liable to forfeiture.

The Court in **Amber Services** (McCombe LJ, Ouseley J concurring) rejected that argument and confirmed that:

> "[16] … it seems to me that by virtue of these provisions the determination of ultimate liability to forfeiture is effected in civil proceedings under Schedule 3 to the 1979 Act. That result follows from section 139(6) … Section 170B(2) is merely one of the provisions in this Act under which such liability has to be decided in this way. In conducting this exercise, as happened in this case, the relevant court will decide in civil proceedings whether the precondition of liability (viz that a person is guilty of an offence under section 170B(1)) is satisfied. Provided that this is the case, as the judge found it to be here, liability to forfeiture and condemnation is established. It seems to me that, provided the court is satisfied to the civil standard that a person, i.e. some person (identified or not) is guilty of an offence under the section liability for forfeiture arises. By its own terms, therefore, the subsection does not require proof of any conviction.".

Thus, where an officer has grounds to suspect that an offence of fraudulent evasion of duty has been committed (whether by the individual traveller or by another), they are entitled to seize any goods involved and, if appropriate, effect secondary seizure of any vehicle used and other items pursuant to section 141(1)(a) and (b) CEMA, respectively.

PART THREE

CONDEMNATION PROCEEDINGS

CHAPTER FIVE

PROVISIONS RELATING TO SEIZURE AND CONDEMNATION PROCEEDINGS

Schedule 3 CEMA 1979

Notice of Seizure

The statutory provisions relating to seizure are set out in Schedule 3 to CEMA and start with the requirement that Notice is given by Border Force to;

> "any person who to their [Border Force's] knowledge was at the time of the seizure the owner or one of the owners" of the item(s) seized" (para 1(1) of Schedule 3),

unless,

> "1(2) …the seizure was made in the presence of:
>
> (a) the person or any person whose offence or suspected offence occasioned the seizure; or
>
> (b) the owner or any of the owners of the thing seized or any servant or agent of his; or
>
> (ba) a person who has (or appears to have) possession or control of the thing being seized; or

(c) in the case of any thing seized on or from any ship or aircraft, the master or commander; or

(d) in the case of any thing seized on or from a vehicle, the driver of the vehicle."

Section 1 of CEMA defines "owner" for the purposes of owners of aircraft or pipelines but does not provide any express clarification so as to deal with the situation where a vehicle is rented or borrowed at the time of a seizure pursuant to section 141(1)(a) i.e. where it is being used to transport goods which are themselves liable to forfeiture. However, section 1 confirms that the term " 'proprietor' in relation to any goods, includes any owner, importer, exporter, shipping or other person for the time being possessed of or beneficially interested in those goods" which suggests that any person possessed of or beneficially interested in an item should be treated as the owner for the purposes of the Act. This interpretation is consistent with, for instance, Road Traffic Act 1989 section 192(1) and Theft Act 1967 section12(7)(b).

There is no requirement as to a timescale for providing the Notice of Seizure and service may be effected by personal delivery, postal service at the usual or last known place of abode or business (or registered office, in the case of a company) of the owner or, if no UK address is known, by publication in the Gazette (para. 2 of Sch. 3).

Equally, there is no requirement for the Notice to provide details of the reasons or grounds for the seizure (in contrast to the requirement for a Notice of Detention under Schedule 2A, see above). This is consistent with the decision of the Supreme Court in **Eastenders** which confirmed that the lawfulness of a decision to seize goods under section 139(1) CEMA is not dependent upon the officer's subjective assessment of the circumstances but on an objective assessment of whether it is liable to forfeiture. Presumably, if it were to be specifically asserted that the seizure was made pursuant to section 139(1A) then the lawfulness of the seizure would be dependent upon whether the officer did have grounds to "reasonably suspect" that the item was liable to forfeiture.

A seizure does not, necessarily, involve the item being physically retained by the Commissioners; it can be allowed to remain where it was seized in which case the "responsible person" (i.e. one of the individuals outlined in para. 1(2) of Sch. 3, see above, or a person the seizing officer reasonably believes to satisfy one of those criteria) is required to prevent the item's unauthorised removal or disposal and, in default, will be liable to a civil penalty under section 9 Finance Act 1994, i.e. equivalent to either the duty due on the item (if any) or, if the item is not subject to duty, the value of the item when it was seized with, in both cases, a minimum penalty of £250 (para 18).

If the responsible person is a revenue trader then, if any item is removed or otherwise disposed of without permission, the Commissioners can seize as "liable to forfeiture" the trader's stock to the value of the item (para 19).

Any person seeking to challenge the seizure on the ground that that item was not, in fact, liable to forfeiture has one month (i.e. one calendar month) from the date of the Notice of Seizure or, if no notice was issued, the date of the seizure (para 3); there is no provision for the extension of time where, for example, a driver does not tell or delays telling the owner of the item or vehicle that it has been seized. The Notice of Claim must be in writing (para 3) and provide the name or address of the person making the claim ("the Claimant") and, if they are "outside the United Kingdom, the name and address of a solicitor in the United Kingdom who is authorised to accept service of process and to act on behalf of the claimant" (para 4(1)).

It follows that a foreign national (or a UK resident who is unable to provide an address) who fails to instruct a UK solicitor cannot make a valid claim, although the First Tier Tribunal Tax Chamber case of **Wnek v Director of Border Force** [2014] 1 CMLR 1357 suggests that the restriction was not proportionate and amounted to discrimination so had to be disapplied in respect of EU citizens.

If no Notice of Claim is made then after one month (from the date of the Notice of Seizure, or if no Notice was issued, the date of seizure) the seized item (or items) is duly "condemned as forfeit" (para 5).

If a Notice of Claim is received then the Commissioners:

> "shall take proceedings for the condemnation of that thing by the court, and if the court finds that the thing was at the time of seizure liable to forfeiture the court shall condemn it as forfeit" (para 6).

The effect of para 6 is severe; it was well established that if the court finds that goods are liable to forfeiture then it must condemn them as forfeit (**De Keyser v British Railway Traffic and Electric Co Ltd** [1936] 1 KB 224 (DC) and any vehicle, etc. used to transport those goods and any other goods found mixed, packed or found with those goods are also condemned (see **R (on the application of Customs and Excise Commissioners) v Helman** [2002] EWHC 2254 (Admin)).

However, **Customs and Excise Commissioners v Newbury** [2003] EWHC 702 (Admin) tempered that severity in respect of items and vehicles, etc. liable to forfeiture pursuant to section 141 (i.e. secondary forfeiture) so as to require that it must be proportionate for those secondary items to be condemned; weighing the public interest, for example, in preventing smuggling, against the rights of the individual involved. Invitations for further consideration of Newbury (see e.g. **Customs and Excise Commissioners v Berriman** [2007] EWHC

1183 (Admin) at para [36]) remained unanswered and it has repeatedly been affirmed in higher courts.

Where an item is condemned as forfeit under para 6 or deemed to be condemned as forfeit under para 5 of the Schedule, para 7 provides that the "forfeiture shall have effect from the date when the liability to forfeiture arose" (i.e. usually the date of the interception).

Condemnation proceedings are civil (as opposed to criminal) and are instituted in the High Court or, more usually, a Magistrates Court (or, in Scotland the Court of Session or the sheriff court, or in Northern Ireland the High Court or a court of summary jurisdiction) (para 8) and, if in the latter court in each jurisdiction, may be instituted:

> "(a) in any such court having jurisdiction in the place where any offence in connection with that thing was committed or where any proceedings for such an offence are instituted; or
>
> (b) in any such court having jurisdiction in the place where the claimant resides or, if the claimant has specified a solicitor under paragraph 4 above [e.g. a foreign national] in the place where that solicitor has his office; or
>
> (c) in any court having jurisdiction in the place where that thing was found, detained or seized or to which it is first brought after being found, detained or seized" (para 9)

The options are not sequential and the reality is that most condemnations are issued and heard in the Magistrates' Court local to where the items were seized i.e. serving the port or airport where the interception took place, and requests for a change of venue to suit the Claimant are rarely successful.

As indicated above, and notwithstanding the reference in para 9(a) to any connected "offence", condemnation proceedings are civil and so are commenced by a "complaint" brought by the seizing authority rather than the claimant (i.e. the individual whose seek to recover their seized items(s) and, pursuant to Section 127(1) of the Magistrates Courts Act 1980, must be brought "within 6 months from the time …the matter of complaint arose". The issue of the timing was considered in HM **Customs & Excise v Venn** [2001] EWHC 1055 (Admin) which determined that the relevant time starts with the Notice of Claim.

The time limit for issuing alternative proceedings in the High Court was also considered in the case of **Gascoyne v Customs & Excise Commissioners** [2003] EWHC 257 (HC) (affirmed on appeal at [2004] EWCA Civ 1162); which confirmed that proceedings could be brought in the High Court more than six months after the Notice of Claim had been served (as section 127 only applies to Magistrates Courts and section 37(2)(b) of the Limitation Act 1980 specifically exempts "any forfeiture proceedings under the customs and excise Acts") although such proceedings could be struck out in the event of an unjustified or oppressive delay or if it had been indicated that condemnation proceedings would not be brought.

The fact that the proceedings are civil also has the effect of removing any entitlement to public funding to assist an individual affected by, for instance, the loss of their family car (**R (on the application of Mudie) v Kent Magistrates Court** [2003] EWCA Civ 237, approving **Goldsmith v Customs and Excise Commissioners** [2001] 1WLR 1673.

Paragraph 10 of the Schedule requires;

> "(1) … the claimant or his solicitor to make oath to confirm that the thing seized was, or was to the best of his

> knowledge and belief, the property of the claimant at the time of the seizure [and] …
>
> (3) If any requirement of this paragraph is not complied with, the court shall give judgment for the Commissioners".

It follows that if the owner fails to attend or cannot swear to ownership (or his solicitor is unable to confirm ownership of the item) at the time of seizure then the Court must condemn the item. If an issue is raised as to ownership, for example, if it appears the claimant acquired the seized item (i.e. either the goods or the vehicle) after the seizure or did not own it at all (e.g. it belonged to a friend at the time) then the Court will order condemnation without hearing further evidence.

In practice the Court will usually be satisfied if the claimant is able to establish that they have were in possession of or had a beneficial interest in the seized item (i.e. they were the "proprietor" as defined in section 1 CEMA of the item rather than the "owner").

Where the owner is a corporate body or a partnership the oath can be given by "the secretary or other duly authorised officer of that body" (or someone authorised by those individuals) or one of the partners or, if the item is jointly owned by more than five individuals who are not partners (e.g. an unincorporated association) by any two of those individuals (para 15).

Paragraph 10(2) provides for the claimant in High Court proceedings to give security for costs in a sum to be determined by the court.

Paragraph 11 makes provision for appeals to the Crown Court against a decision in the Magistrates Court (see below) or to the High Court by way of case stated, and paragraph 12 provides that pending the outcome of any appeal the item(s) subject of the appeal shall be retained by the Commissioners (Border Force).

Paragraph 13 of the Schedule confirms that;

> "the fact, form and manner of the seizure shall be taken to have been set forth in the process [i.e. the Complaint] without any further evidence thereof, unless the contrary is proved",

so that the burden of proof shifts onto the claimant if an issue is raised about the basis of the initial seizure, for example, the statutory provision relied upon.. This accords with section 154 of the Act which imposes a "reverse burden" on the individual claiming the goods to show that, for instance, duty had been paid when the goods had been purchased or that to items were not subject to any prohibition or restriction at that time (e.g. cannisters of nitrous oxide prior to its reclassification as a class C drug).

Condemnation of an item is achieved by (and can be proved by production of) an "order or certificate of condemnation or a certified copy thereof" (para 14).

Paragraph 16 allows the Commissioners, pending determination of the condemnation proceedings, to deliver up the item(s) to the claimant, upon payment of "a sum not exceeding ....the value of the thing" (including any unpaid duty) or, if the item is perishable or living, they may "sell or destroy it" (para 16).

If the item is subsequently found not to have been liable to forfeiture and so is not condemned then the Commissioners are required (if the claimant makes a demand) to compensate them to the value of the item at the time of seizure, less any unpaid duty (para 17). In the event of a dispute regarding the market value of an item provision is made for determination of the issue by a referee appointed by the Lord Chanceller in conjunction with a nominee of the Lord Chief Justice, or equivalent in Scotland or Northern Ireland (para 17(5)-(8)).

In practice excise goods such as tobacco or alcohol which have been seized are routinely destroyed and, in the event they are not condemned, compensation is paid, whereas vehicles (as non-perishable) are stored and will be made available for collection, albeit that they may well have reduced in value between seizure and the determination of the condemnation proceedings.

CHAPTER SIX

CONDEMNATION PROCEEDINGS

Complaint Process

As previously indicated, condemnation proceedings are confirmed in Schedule 3 (para 8) as being civil (and see **Mudie**, supra) and the procedure in such situations is governed by the provisions of the Magistrates Courts Act 1980 ("MCA") Part II, i.e. for present purposes, sections 51 to 58 and 64. Unhelpfully, the MCA refers to the parties as the Complainant (i.e. party seeking the condemnation order) and the "defendant" (when it should be "the claimant" as they are the individual who issued the notice of claim which gives rise to the proceedings).

The MCA sets out the power of the Court to issue the summons (section 51), hear the complaint (section 52), adjourn or stay proceedings (section 54), proceed in the absence of a "defendant" (section 55), to dismiss the complaint if the "defendant" attends but the complainant does not attend (section 56) or if neither party attends (section 57) or to transfer the matter to another magistrates court (section 58) and to award costs (section 64 – see Chapter 8, **Costs and Compensation**, below).

Section 121 of the MCA provides that (unless a deputy district judge or a district judge is dealing with the matter) the Magistrates Court dealing with condemnation proceedings must be comprised of at least two and not more than three magistrates and the hearing must be conducted in public.

It is not unusual for there to be parallel criminal proceedings arising out of the same or connected circumstances as condemnation proceeding. A criminal defendant has a right not to incriminate himself whereas in civil proceedings he may be obliged to give evidence to justify his claim that the seized items were not liable to forfeiture or (particularly in the case of a secondary forfeiture) that it was not proportionate for the items to be condemned. In such a situation the appropriate course would be for the civil proceedings to be adjourned or stayed pending the outcome of the criminal matter(s) – see **R v Payton** [2006] EWCA Crim 1226.

If there are ongoing or concurrent criminal proceedings or investigations it may be necessary for the Complainant to make a Public Interest Immunity ("PII") application to withhold or exclude material the disclosure of which would prejudice those other matters; such applications are rare (particularly given the effective presumption that civil proceedings will be stayed pending the determination of any connected criminal matters).

(No) Rules of Procedure

Despite the provisions in the MCA for the Magistrates' Court to deal with various civil proceedings, there are no specific rules within the Magistrates Courts Rules 1981 for the usual processes of disclosure, exchange of witness statements or the arrangements for the preparation of hearing bundles: the Civil Procedure Rules 1989 ("CPR") do not apply to Magistrates courts (see CPR 2.1) and, obviously, the Criminal Procedure Rules 2015 ("CrimPR") do not apply to civil proceedings (see CrimPR 2.1(1)(a)).

As a result, condemnation proceedings fall between the various statutory regimes and the Court has to fall back in its implicit jurisdiction – see Hickinbottom J in **R (on the application of V) v**

Asylum and Immigration Tribunal [2009] EWHC 1902 (Admin) at [30]:

> "… in respect of any tribunal with a judicial function, it must be assumed (at least in the absence of the clearest wording) that Parliament intended the tribunal to deal with cases fairly and justly: and, consequently, provisions that are not incompatible with the express rules can be readily implied insofar as they are necessary for achieving fairness and justice"

and **R (on the application of Chief Constable of Nottinghamshire Police) v Nottingham Magistrates Court** [2009] EWHC 3182 (Admin) where Moses LJ, at para 33, confirmed (and Hickinbottom J agreed, at para 52) that Hickinbottom J in **V** had;

> "dismantled any superstition that a statutory tribunal, or for that matter a statutory court such as the magistrates had any inherent jurisdiction"

First Hearing

In practice and assuming the matter is to be contested the Court will usually give directions at a first hearing for the onward progression of the case providing for the exchange of statements and evidence either simultaneously (in a straightforward case where the issues are clear) or sequentially (if the matter is more involved) in advance of the date set for trial. The late provision of evidence, by either side, will often result in an application for an adjournment and should be avoided.

Given the requirement under para 10(1) of Schedule 3 of CEMA for the owner of the items in dispute to swear to ownership it is often most efficient for this to be dealt with at the first hearing (if the

Claimant is unable to swear to ownership then the items are immediately condemned).

Where there is an issue as to ownership at the time of the seizure (e.g. where a car was being borrowed by the driver at the time of interception and, following or as a result of the seizure, the driver has subsequently purchased the car and then makes a claim for its return) it may be that the act of swearing to ownership can result in cross-examination or questions from the Bench, but see above regarding the wider reading of "owner" as "proprietor" (i.e. "being possessed of or beneficially interested in [the goods") pursuant to section 1 CEMA.

Section 123 Magistrates Courts Act 1980 and associated case law gives a wide discretion to permit the amendment of a complaint (or information) and prevents objection being taken to

> "any defect … in substance or form, or for any variance between it and the evidence adduced on behalf of the … complainant at the hearing of the information or complaint" (section 123(1)),

save that if any variance,

> "is such that the defendant has been misled by the variance, the court shall, on the application of the defendant, adjourn the hearing" (section 123(2)).

Absence of Parties

In the event that the Claimant (individual) does not attend Court at the appointed date and time then, subject to the court being satisfied that they were aware of the proceedings and the hearing, the Court can proceed in their absence or may adjourn (and/or, if the complaint is substantiated on oath, issue a warrant for the arrest of the Claimant, although this is rarely done in condemnation proceedings where it is more effective simply to proceed to condemn the item(s) and see if an appeal is lodged).

If the Claimant attends but the Complainant (Border Force) does not then the complaint may be dismissed or, if evidence has previously been received, proceed in the Complainant's absence. If neither party attends the court may dismiss the complaint or adjourn the proceedings. The relevant statutory provisions can be found at sections 54 to 57 of the Magistrates Courts Act 1980.

Burden and Standard of Proof

As provided by para 8 of Schedule 3, condemnation proceedings are civil so the relevant standard of proof is the balance of probabilities (i.e. more likely than not) but this is,

> "… flexible in its application. In particular, the more serious the allegation or the more serious the consequences if the allegation is proved, the stronger must be the evidence before a court will find the allegation proved on the balance of probabilities. Thus, the flexibility of the standard lies not in any adjustment to the degree of probability required for the allegation to be proved, such that a more serious allegation has to be proved to a higher degree of probability, but in the strength or quality of the evidence that will, in practice, be required for an allegation to be proved on the balance of probabilities" (Richards LJ **in R (N) v Mental Health Tribunal** [2005] EWCA Civ 1605 at para 62).

That said, the proceedings are "in rem", i.e. in respect of the things alleged to be liable to forfeiture, rather than necessarily involving any specific allegation of misconduct or wrongdoing on the part of the Claimant (**R (Mudie) v Dover Magistrates Court** [2003] EWCA Civ 237, approving **Goldsmith v Commissioners of Customs and Excise** [2001] EWHC Admin 285) and the individual is not being exposed to the risk of any fine or other financial penalty (see **Air Canada v UK** (1995) 20 EHRR 150 where an aircraft was seized following the discovery of drugs amongst its load but was later restored to the company on payment of £50,000).

The loss of the value of the goods or items involved does not amount to a penalty, although it may be relevant to the issue of the proportionality of their condemnation. Similarly, the inevitable risk of an adverse costs order as a result of the proceedings does not amount to a penalty.

Because the focus is on the item(s) the identity of the Claimant (save as "owner" of the goods subject to the claim) is not a relevant factor – see **Denton v John Lister Ltd** [1971] 3 All ER 669, decided under previous legislation.

Notwithstanding the above, section 154(2) CEMA provides a reverse burden of proof in respect of certain matters, namely:

> "Where in any proceedings relating to Revenue and Customs any question arises as to the place in which any goods have been brought or as to whether or not-
>
> (a) any duty has been paid or secured in respect of any goods; or
>
> (b) any goods or other things whatsoever are of the description or nature alleged in the information, writ or other process; or

> (c) any goods have been lawfully imported or lawfully unloaded from any ship, aircraft or railway vehicle; or
>
> (d) any goods have been lawfully loaded into any ship, aircraft or railway vehicle or lawfully exported or were lawfully waterborne; or
>
> (e) any goods were lawfully brought to any place for the purpose of being loaded into any ship, aircraft or railway vehicle or exported; or
>
> (f) any goods are or were subject to any prohibition of or restriction on their importation or exportation,
>
> then, where those proceedings are brought by or against the Commissioners ... the burden of proof shall lie upon the other party to the proceedings.",

so that the Claimant will bear the burden of proving (to the civil standard) that, for example, duty had been paid on goods and/or that whether there is a prohibition or restriction on importation of the goods.

Because the proceedings do not involve the determination of any criminal charges the presumption of innocence under Article 6(2) of the Convention on Human Rights (via the Human Rights Act 1998) has no application in condemnation proceedings; alternatively, any burden placed on the individual was proportionate, reasonable and justified: (**Goldsmith v Customs and Excise Commissioners** [2001] EWHC Admin 285).

Reason for Interception

The reason for the interception and/or the search of the individual is irrelevant as regards the condemnation proceedings, see **R (Hoverspeed Ltd) v Customs and Excise Commissioners** [2002] EWCA Civ 1804, particularly Mance LJ's judgment:

> "44. … the powers of seizure conferred by sections 49(1)(a), 141(1) and 139(1) of and Schedule 3 to CEMA are not made dependent upon the exercise of any power to stop and search provided in any other sections, such as sections 163 and 163A. The object in undertaking a search will be to look for unlawfully held goods, but that does not mean that the validity of any seizure of such goods is conditional upon the legitimacy of the search. The power to seize is exercisable even when no search is necessary – to take an obvious example, if a person carrying goods liable to forfeiture puts them on the ground, discards them, or leaves or hides them in some other place to which Customs have access. The power is not exercisable under any warrant or by reference to any criterion, save that the goods are 'liable to forfeiture'. Further, if the power is exercised, and its exercise is challenged in condemnation proceedings, the condemnation court *must* condemn the goods if it finds that they were liable to forfeiture: paragraph 6 of Schedule 3 to CEMA.
>
> 45. … If proceedings in which an issue arose whether goods were 'liable to forfeiture' were viewed as criminal, it would need to be determined whether answers obtained from or statements made by a traveller during the course of an illegal check could properly be used to incriminate. Whatever the position in that regard, we believe that English law, fortified by the European Convention on

> Human Rights, would ensure that no unfairness resulted from an unlawful check. We do not however see any unfairness in the seizure of goods liable to forfeiture, even though their presence happens only to be discovered in the course of an unlawful check. That may be bad luck, but it is not unfair."

Hearsay Evidence

The Magistrates Courts (Hearsay in Civil Proceedings) Rules 1999 and the Civil Evidence Act 1995 set out the detailed procedure for the provision of hearsay notices not less than 21 days before the date fixed for hearing (rule 3(1)) or as ordered by the Court (rule 3(2)) and the requirements of such a Notice (rule 3(4)), the procedure to applying to call the witness to give evidence (rule 4) within 7 days of receipt of a hearsay notice in order to challenge their credibility (rule 5) and the requirements for service of any such notices (rule 6).

However, a failure to follow the rules does not affect the admissibility of that hearsay evidence (Civil Evidence Act section 2(4)) but may impact the weight to be given to it and can be taken into account when the court is exercising "its powers with respect to the course of proceedings and costs".

When determining the weight to be given to hearsay evidence, the court "shall have regards to any circumstances from which any inference can reasonably be drawn as to the reliability or otherwise of the evidence" (section 4(1)) and may have regard to various matters set out in section 4(2)(a) to (f), i.e. whether it would be reasonable and practicable to produce the maker of the original statement as a witness; whether the original statement was made contemporaneously, involved multiple hearsay, was edited or made in collaboration with another; and/or whether any person involved had an ulterior motive or there was any suggestion of an attempt to prevent proper evaluation of the evidence.

On appeal to the Crown Court, while the Magistrates Court (Hearsay in Civil Proceedings) Rules 1999 do not apply to the Crown Court, in **R v W** [2006] EWCA Crim 686 the Court of Appeal, dealing with an appeal regarding an Anti-Social Behaviour Order, faced with the fact that no procedural rules applied in the Crown Court for dealing with a civil matter and concerned to ensure that the defendant was aware of the case he faced and had a proper opportunity to challenge the evidence against him, stated that:

> "The 1999 Rules make provision for all this and we will presume that, by analogy, the principles set out in those rules should have been followed in this case" (Aikens J at para 37).

Previous convictions of a party (or, indeed, their acquittal In previous criminal proceedings) may be relevant and admissible in condemnation proceedings and may be evidenced by production of a certificate of conviction pursuant to sections 11 and 12 of the Civil Evidence Act 1968 and the provisions relating to evidence of bad character and the restrictions on drawing adverse inferences from a party's refusal to give evidence applicable in criminal proceedings do not apply to condemnation hearings.

<u>Substantive Hearing</u>

The procedure at the substantive hearing of a complaint is set out in the Magistrates Courts Rules 1981 at rule 14, which states:

> "(1) On the hearing of a complaint, except where the court determines under section 53(3) of the Act of 1980 to make the order with the consent of the defendant

without hearing evidence, the complainant shall call his evidence, and before doing so may address the court.

(2) At the conclusion of the evidence for the complainant the defendant may address the court, whether or not he afterwards calls evidence.

(3) At the conclusion of the evidence, if any, for the defence, the complainant may call evidence to rebut that evidence.

(4) At the conclusion of the evidence for the defence and the evidence, if any, in rebuttal, the defendant may address the court if he has not already done so.

(5) Either party may, with the leave of the court, address the court a second time, but where the court grants leave to one party it shall not refuse leave to the other.

(6) Where the defendant obtains leave to address the court for a second time his second address shall be made before the second address, if any, of the complainant."

As indicated above, the Complainant is permitted to open its case (at (1) above) but will not necessarily (or usually) be afforded a second opportunity to address the Court; it follows that when "opening" the case the Complainant should set out its case fully as regards both the relevant law and the facts.

There is therefore, inevitably, the risk that fresh information will be presented in the course of the live evidence, particularly if a Claimant is unrepresented and/or has not provided a written statement in accordance with any directions but is nevertheless permitted to give oral evidence, but the opportunity for the Complainant to call rebuttal evidence and/or to seek leave to address the court a second time (in closing) is available.

Submission of No Case to Answer

At the conclusion of the Complainant's evidence (after (1) above) it is open to the Claimant to make a "submission of no case to answer" and invite the Court to find in the Claimant's favour purely on the basis of the evidence it has heard from the Complainant's witness(es), but before doing so they should be "put to their election", i.e. expressly given the choice of making such a submission or calling evidence.

If they are not put to their election then, regardless of the outcome of their submission, they would be entitled to call further evidence (**Jones v Metcalfe** [1967] 3 All ER 205) but if they elect to make a submission and fail then they are not permitted to call any further evidence; see **Boyce v Wyatt Engineering** [2001] EWCA Civ 692:

> "... where a defendant is put to his election, that is the end of the matter as regards evidence. The judge will not hear any further evidence which might give cause to reconsider findings made on the basis of the claimant's case alone. The case either fails or succeeds, even on appeal." (Mance LJ at para 4).

It is not clear how this, widely accepted, principle tallies with the wording of Rule 14(2), above, i.e. that "the defendant may address the court, whether or not he afterwards calls evidence".

Closing Submission(s)

The procedure also allows the Claimant to address the Court in opening (at (2) above) but if it does there is no guarantee they will be permitted to make a second address (at (4) and (5) above); the Claimant usually opts to keep their powder dry and save any address for closing submissions.

In any event either party may address the Court on a point of law at any stage (and the other will be given a right of reply).

The Decision

At the conclusion of the evidence (and any further submissions) the Court will usually retire to reach its decision and should provide oral reasons for its decision when handing down judgment and, in due course, a written record of the decision will be made in the Court's register.

Often the Complainant authority will have standard Orders to be signed by the Court in the event that either the Condemnation Order is made or there is an Order for the Dismissal of the Complaint (in which case the order will usually include a term certifying that there were reasonable grounds for the original seizure of the item(s) and referring to section 144 CEMA – see Chapter 8, **Costs and Compensation,** below).

Power to set Aside

Although the power for the Magistrates Court to set aside decisions or to reopen proceedings under section 142 Magistrates Courts Act 1980 is expressly limited to criminal proceedings it has been held in **Liverpool City Council v Pleroma Distribution Ltd** [2002] EWHC

2467 (Admin) that the Court can do the same in civil proceedings (see also the discussion regarding **R (on the application of V) v Asylum and Immigration Tribunal** and **R (on the application of Chief Constable of Nottinghamshire Police) v Nottingham Magistrates Court** in the context of Procedure, above).

The three criteria to be considered when assessing an application to set aside a decision are (i) whether there is a genuine and arguable issue, (ii) the order must be the result of a "substantial procedural error, defect or mishap" and (iii) the application must be made promptly once the applicant becomes aware of the decision or order; Stanley Burnton J in **Brighton and Hove Council v Brighton and Hove Justices** [2004] EWHC 1800 Admin at para 31.

CHAPTER SEVEN

APPEALING A CONDEMNATION DECISION

Appeal to the Crown Court

Para 11 of Schedule 3 of CEMA provides for the option of an appeal to the Crown Court by either party from the Magistrates Court proceedings and the appeal is by way of re-hearing (section 79(3) Senior Courts Act 1981). The procedure for making the appeal is set out in the Crown Court Rules 1982 at rule 7; any appeal should be made within 21 days of the decision being appealed (as previously indicated, the provisions for appeal to the Crown Court in the Criminal Procedure Rules at do not apply so it is not "not more than 15 business days" under Crim PR 32.2(2)(b)) although there is scope for that to be extended by written application to the Crown Court (Rule 7(6)).

In the event that an extension of time is allowed the Judge should give reasons for so doing **R (Customs and Excise Commissioners) v Maidstone Crown Court** [2004] EWHC 1459 (Admin) and, in the event that the decision is made on the basis of a factual or legal error, the court may exercise its inherent jurisdiction to set aside that decision (**R (UKBA) v Portsmouth Crown Court** [2011] EWHC 3517 (Admin))

As the hearing in the Crown Court is a re hearing it is open to either party to adduce new evidence (**Sagnata Investments v Norwich Corporation** [1971] 2 QB 614 (CA))

The Crown Court hearing the appeal will consist of a Crown Court Judge (or Recorder or High Court Judge) and "not less than two and not more than four justices of the peace" who were not involved in the decision being appealed (Senior Courts Act 1981 section 74(1)); while CrimPR 34.11(2)(a) allows for the Crown Court Judge to sit with a single justice if to do otherwise would unreasonably delay the start of the case or if, once the appeal has commenced, one of the magistrates is absent, by virtue of CrimPR 2.1(1) that dispensation is not available where the Court is sitting in its civil jurisdiction.

Appeal by way of Case Stated

Section 111(1) Magistrates Courts Act 1980 provides that:

> "Any person who was a party to any proceeding before a magistrates' court or is aggrieved by the conviction, order, determination or other proceeding of the court may question the proceeding on the ground that it is wrong in law or is in excess of jurisdiction by applying to the justices composing the court to state a case for the opinion of the High Court on the question of law or jurisdiction involved …"

In addition, the right to apply to state a case is specifically reserved in para 11 of Schedule 3 of CEMA. Any such application must be made within 21 days of the decision being challenged (section 111(2)) and the procedure for such an application is set out in the Civil Procedure Rules at CPR52 (and Practice Direction 52E).

CHAPTER EIGHT

COSTS AND COMPENSATION

Section 64 of the Magistrates Courts Act 1980 provides that:

> "(1) On the hearing of a complaint, a magistrates' court shall have power in its discretion to make such order as to costs-
>
> > (a) on making the order for which the complaint is made, to be paid by the defendant to the complainant;
> >
> > (b) on dismissing the complaint, to be paid by the complainant to the defendant,
>
> as it thinks just and reasonable …
>
> (2) The amount of any sum ordered to be paid under subsection (1) shall be specified in the order, or order of dismissal, as the case may be.
>
> (3) Costs ordered to be paid under this section shall be enforceable as a civil debt."

It follows that any costs application (and order) should be made at the same time as the condemnation or dismissal; as indicated above, there are no procedural rules e.g. relating to service of costs schedules, but ideally parties should exchange schedules in advance and be ready to deal with any costs application at the conclusion of the substantive hearing.

The Magistrates Court do not need to make any order relating to the terms of payment (i.e. the period for or amount of payment by instalments) and the usual rule for civil orders, including orders for costs, is that payment should be made within 14 days of the order (under CPR 40.11).

Notwithstanding the level playing field created by section 64(1), i.e. the successful party may recover its costs, the case of **R (Perinpanathan) v City of Westminster Magistrates Court** [2010] EWCA Civ 40 (dealing with a cash forfeiture under the Proceeds of Crime Act 2002) was authority for the proposition that:

> "where the party opposing the order sought by the public authority has been successful, in relation to costs the starting point and default position is that no order should be made" (Stanley Burnton LJ in **Perinpanathan** at [40] – see below).

The path to that principle was derived from **City of Bradford DC v Booth** (2000) 164 JP 485 (which was approved by the Court of Appeal in **Baxendale-Walker v Law Society** [2007] EWCA Civ 233) which stated:

> "where a complainant has successfully challenged before justices an administrative decision made by a police or regulatory authority acting honestly, reasonably, properly and on grounds that reasonably appeared to be sound, in exercise of its public duty, the court should consider, in addition to any other relevant fact or circumstances, both (i) the financial prejudice to the particular complainant in the particular circumstances if an order for costs is not

made in his favour; and (ii) the need to encourage public authorities to make and stand by honest, reasonable and apparently sound administrative decisions made in the public interest without fear of exposure to undue financial prejudice if the decision is successfully challenged" (Lord Bingham CJ at page 491 of **Bradford**)

Stanley Burnton LJ in **Perinpanathan** stated:

> "[40] I derive the following propositions from the authorities...
>
> > (1) ... the principle in [Bradford] is binding on this court ...
> >
> > (2) ... the principle is applicable to disciplinary proceedings before tribunals at first instance brought by public authorities acting in the public interest [Baxendale-Walker] ...
> >
> > (3) Whether the principle should be applied in other contexts will depend on the substantive legislative framework and the applicable procedural provisions.
> >
> > (4) The principle does not apply in proceedings to which the CPR [Civil Procedure Rules 1998] apply.
> >
> > (5) Where the principle applies, and the party opposing the order sought by the public authority has been successful, in relation to costs the starting point and default position is that no order should be made.
> >
> > (6) A successful private party to proceedings to which the principle applies may none the less be

> awarded all or part of his costs if the conduct of the public authority in question justifies it.
>
> (7) Other facts relevant to the exercise of the discretion conferred by the applicable procedural rules may also justify an order for costs. It would not be sensible to try exhaustively to define such matters, and I do not propose to do so.

[41] Lord Bingham CJ stated that financial prejudice to the private party may justify an order for costs in his favour. I think it clear that the financial prejudice necessarily involved in litigation would not normally justify an order. If that were not so, an order would be made in every case in which a successful private party incurred legal costs. Lord Bingham CJ had in mind a case in which the successful private party would suffer substantial hardship is no order for costs were made in his favour.

[42] … Ultimately, the duty of the magistrates' court is to make such order as to costs as is just and reasonable, subject to the constraint imposed by s64.".

Lord Neuberger MR in **Perinpanathan** stated:

"[77] The effect of our decision is that a person in the position of the appellant, who has done nothing wrong, may normally not be able to recover the costs of vindicating her rights against the police in proceedings under s298 of the 2002 Act, where the police have behaved reasonably. In my view, this means that magistrates should exercise particular care when considering whether the police have acted reasonably in a

> case where there is an application for costs against them under s64. It would be wrong to invoke the wisdom of hindsight or to set too exacting a standard, but, particularly given the understandable resentment felt by a person in the position of the appellant if no order for costs is made, and the general standards of behaviour that can properly be expected from the police, it must be right to scrutinise their behaviour in relation to the seizure, the detention, and the confiscation proceedings, with some care when deciding whether they acted reasonably and properly.".

The **Booth** line of authorities were considered in **Competition and Markets Authority v Flynn Pharma Ltd** [2022] UKSC 14 where Lady Rose JSC found that:

> "[97] … there is no generally applicable principle that all public bodies should enjoy a protected status as parties to litigation where they lose a case which they have brought or defended in the exercise of their public functions in the public interest. The principle supported by the Booth line of cases is, rather, that where a public body is unsuccessful in proceedings, an important factor that a court or tribunal exercising an apparently unfettered discretion should take into account is the risk that there will be a chilling effect on the conduct of the public body, if costs orders are routinely made against it in those kinds of proceedings, even where the body has acted reasonably in bringing or defending the application. This does not mean that a court has to consider the point afresh each time it exercises its discretion in, for example, a case where a local authority loses a licensing appeal or every time the magistrates dismiss an application brought by the police. The assessment that, in the kinds of proceedings dealt with

> directly in Booth, Baxendale-Walker and Perinpanathan, there is a general risk of a chilling effect applies to the kinds of proceedings in which those cases were decided and to analogous proceedings.
>
> [98] … Whether there is a real risk of such a chilling effect depends on the facts and circumstances of the public body in question and the nature of the decision which it is defending – it cannot be assumed to exist. Further in my judgment, the assessment as to whether a chilling effect is sufficiently plausible to justify a starting point of no order as to costs in a particular jurisdiction is an assessment best made by the court or tribunal in question, subject to the supervisory jurisdiction of the appellate courts."

The effect of **Flynn Pharma** may be that costs awards in favour of successful Claimants become more frequent but, historically, the fact that a Claimant was unlikely to recover their costs in condemnation proceedings was a substantial factor when determining the economics of pursuing a claim and whether "the game was worth the candle". No doubt there will be close examination of the conduct of both parties (upon interception, during any correspondence and in the course of the proceedings) when any costs application is to be determined.

Compensation

While paras 16 and 17 of Schedule 3 make provision for the delivery up of items pending determination of condemnation proceedings, the destruction of perishable items and the payment of compensation if the thing delivered up or destroyed is found not to have been liable to forfeiture at the time of seizure, if the complaint is dismissed there is no provision for compensation to be payable to the Claimant; the item(s) will simply be returned.

Given that condemnation proceedings can take a considerable period to be concluded this may mean that, for instance, a vehicle seized because it was being used to transport other goods which were liable to forfeiture may have been detained and stored (in the open air) and the Claimant will have been deprived of the use of it for some time and it may not be roadworthy when it is returned (or, more accurately, the claimant is allowed to collect it).

Notwithstanding that the Claimant may have suffered loss as a result of the detention of the item, section 144 CEMA provides protection against any civil claim by the successful claimant if the Court has certified that there were "reasonable grounds for the seizure" in the first instance (or if the court dealing with the subsequent claim finds that there were "reasonable grounds for seizing or detaining" the item(s)).

Section 144 CEMA

> "(1) Where, in any proceedings for the condemnation of any thing seized as liable to forfeiture under the customs and excise Acts, judgment is given for the claimant, the court may, as it sees fit, certify that there were reasonable grounds for the seizure.
>
> (2) Where any proceedings, whether civil or criminal, are brought against the Commissioners, a law officer of the Crown or any person authorised by or under the Customs and Excise Acts 1979 to seize or detain any thing liable to forfeiture under the customs and excise Acts on account of the seizure or detention of any thing, and judgment is given for the plaintiff or prosecutor, then if either-
>
> > (a) a certificate relating to the seizure has been granted under subsection (1) above; or

> (b) the court is satisfied that there were reasonable grounds for seizing or detaining that thing under the customs and excise Acts,
>
> the plaintiff or prosecutor shall not be entitled to recover any damages or costs and the defendant shall not be liable to any punishment.
>
> (3) Nothing in subsection (2) above shall effect any right of any person to the return of the thing seized or detained or to compensation in respect of any damage to the thing or in respect of the destruction thereof.
>
> (4) Any certificate under subsection (1) above may be proved by the production of either the original certificate or a certified copy thereof purporting to be signed by an officer of the court by which it was granted.".

Section 144(1) requires that the Court determine whether it sees fit to certify that there were reasonable grounds for seizure; there is, therefore, an element of discretion and the court may decide not to so certify (e.g. if it is not satisfied, to the civil standard, that there were reasonable grounds).

Any other Court considering the point (i.e. under section 144(2)) can, presumably, come to its own conclusion about the grounds for seizure but where a court dealing with a condemnation hearing has refused to give a section 144 certificate this will, no doubt, factor into the determination of whether the second court "is satisfied that there were reasonable grounds for seizing or detaining" the thing(s).

It is not clear whether the "damage to the thing" which can result in compensation under section 144(3) above, includes damage by reason of storage and/or the passage of time; it is likely that any litigation on point has usually not been considered economically worthwhile.

The determination of the market value of any items destroyed pursuant to paras 16 and 17 of Schedule 3 was considered in **R (Revenue and Customs Commissioners) v Machell** [2005] EWHC 2593 (Admin) where it was held that, while there was no lawful market in the UK for Belgian duty-paid cigarettes, Stanley Burnton J at para 31. considered

> "it necessary to strive against concluding that a market value of goods lawfully purchased is nil ... the market value of cigarettes bought in retail quantities in Belgium is their retail price in Belgium",

(as opposed to the price Mr Machell hoped to achieve for the same cigarettes in the UK).

The same case determined that Mr Machell was not entitled to recover his travel costs in respect of his trip to purchase the excise goods and, in respect of a quantity of alcohol purchased at the same time which was destroyed in error by Customs as "perishable", the referee appointed under para 17(4) had

> "no jurisdiction to determine the market value of goods (other than a living creature) seized under CEMA and destroyed which were not, in the opinion of customs, of a perishable nature" (para 39(b)).

CHAPTER NINE

PROPORTIONALITY

Customs and Excise Commissioners v Newbury [2003] EWHC 702 (Admin) confirms the relevance of the issue of proportionality when dealing with liability to forfeiture under CEMA and the operation of section 141 of CEMA in condemnation proceedings and deserves detailed analysis.

Mr Newbury and three friends, but not Mrs Newbury, travelled to France in Mrs Newbury's car, and purchased excise goods to bring back to the UK. Mr Newbury had informed his friends that they should only bring back goods for their own consumption or as gifts (within the definition of "personal use" under the regime at the time). One of the friends (Mrs Reed) however purchased tobacco and cigarettes for her daughter and son-in-law with money they had given her for the purpose, so that the goods were not for Mrs Reed's personal use (see Chapter 3, **Excise Goods and Personal Allowance** above) and, when questioned by a Customs Officer, she told the officer about the arrangement. As a result, Mrs Reed's tobacco and cigarettes (1.5 kg of tobacco and 600 cigarettes) were seized as was Mrs Newbury's car and all the goods in the car (totalling 8 kg tobacco and 3,200 cigarettes along with other excise goods), including Mr Newbury's. The goods had a value of about £400 and the car was worth £3,000.

Mr Newbury challenged the seizure and the matter was heard by Magistrates who condemned the goods of Mrs Reed under section 49(1) CEMA along with Mrs Newbury's car and Mr Newbury's goods under section 141(1)(a) and (b) CEMA, respectively. The Crown Court allowed his appeal and "Customs" appealed by way of case stated.

The three questions posed for the Divisional Court were:

> (i) "whether liability to forfeiture depended on the lawfulness of the seizure, which, in turn depended on the lawfulness of the initial interception of the travellers" (para [5]) – a specific point which by the time of the appeal in Newbury had been decided in the Hoverspeed case (**R (Hoverspeed Ltd) v Customs and Excise Commissioners** [2002] EWCA Civ 1804): it did not,
>
> (ii) "whether excise good are liable to forfeiture in a case where they are imported without payment of duty and the imported or holder of the goods holds them not for herself, but for others who have given her the money to buy them" (para [6] – Mrs Reed's situation), and
>
> (iii) "whether, notwithstanding the apparently mandatory terms of s 141 of and para 6 of Sch 3 to [CEMA], the court has a residual discretion not to order the condemnation of a thing which is liable to forfeiture, if it considers it disproportionate to do so." (para [7]).

The Divisional Court (Hale J, at that time) stated:

> "[12] ... The right conferred by article 8 [relating to importation for "own use"] is not simply a right not to pay United Kingdom duty on the goods. It must encompass a right to import those goods without paying that duty. When a load of goods is brought into the country in circumstances where customs officers have reasonable suspicions which they wish to investigate, temporary seizure may well be justified. But the court is then charged with determining the facts with a view to deciding whether the goods are in fact liable to forfeiture. Once the court is

satisfied as to which goods a person was himself bringing in for his own use then there is no liability to duty and no need at all for his goods to be forfeit in order to enforce any liability to duty upon those goods. The argument, however, is that it may be necessary to do so in order to enforce the liability to duty of other goods found in the same vehicle. At this point the Community law concept of proportionality becomes relevant. In **Louloudakis v Ellinko Dimosio** (Case C-262-99) [2001] ECR I-5547, 5596, para 67, it was recognised that as penalties were not harmonised within the Community it remained open to member states to choose the penalties which seem appropriate to them.

> 'They must, however, exercise that power in accordance with Community law and its general principles, and consequently with the principle of proportionality … The administrative measures or penalties must not go beyond what is strictly necessary for the objectives pursued and a penalty must not be so disproportionate to the gravity of the infringement that it becomes an obstacle to the freedoms enshrined in the Treaty …'

[13] In this case, the court also found that Mr Newbury had specifically warned his passengers that they must only bring goods in for their own consumption or as gifts. His evidence was that he did not know about Mrs Reed's arrangements. It cannot be necessary to forfeit his goods in order to enforce her liabilities. To do so is in those circumstances indeed an obstacle to the freedoms enshrined in the Treaty and an unjustified interference with his rights under Community law. Indeed it might also be a disproportionate interference with his rights

under the Convention, but that raises rather different issues which are also relevant to the forfeiture of Mrs Newbury's car.

[21] …If section 7(1)(b) of the [Human Rights Act 1998] is to have any meaning, how can a court which is seized of the issue of whether property is liable to confiscation by the state not have a duty to consider whether such liability would be in breach of the owner's Convention rights? If it would be, the court cannot condemn the property: it would itself be acting in breach of Convention rights. It is not compelled by CEMA to do so because the concept of liability to forfeiture is capable of incorporating more recently enacted Convention rights.

[22] The argument that the condemnation and restoration procedures, taken as a whole, are sufficient to provide 'full jurisdiction' for the purpose of article 6 of the Convention does not meet the point that seizure and condemnation are themselves acts of interference with the peaceful enjoyment of property and therefore acts incompatible with Convention rights if forfeiture is disproportionate. It is not sufficient to wait until an owner seeks a review and then exercises his right of appeal [in restoration proceedings]. The right to peaceful enjoyment is engaged from the moment of seizure and continues thereafter. The initial act of seizure may not be disproportionate because the commissioners are entitled to investigate. But the interference should cease once an opportunity is available properly to consider whether it complies with Convention rights. The court should not be asked or expected to make an order which is not only in breach of those rights in itself but also legitimates continuing breach by the

> commissioners unless and until the review process takes place.
>
> [23] However, section 7 of the 1998 Act does not give the court any wider powers than it already has: see section 8(1). Here, the court's powers are 'all or nothing'. So the court can only refuse to condemn if to forfeit at all would be disproportionate. In this case, where only one passenger was making the sort of non-commercial but not necessarily permitted import contemplated by **Lindsay v Customs and Excise Commissioners** [2002] EWCA Civ 267 and neither the car owner nor the car driver knew about it, the Crown Court was clearly entitled to find that any forfeiture was disproportionate. Intermediate cases where forfeiture would not be proportionate if terms were imposed may have to be left to the more sensitive powers of the commissioners and the tribunal.".

The Court also confirmed, in respect of Mrs Reed's goods (i.e. question (ii) above) that because she had been given the money for the purchase the goods were not for her personal use and were liable to forfeiture notwithstanding the lack of any profit on her part (applying the decision in **R v Customs and Excise Commissioners, ex parte EMU Tabac SARL (Imperial Tobacco intervening)** Case C-296/95 [1998] ECR I-1605 which had been approved in the Court of Appeal's decision in **R (Hoverspeed) v Customs and Excise Commissioners** [2002] EWCA Civ 1804.

In respect of question (iii) above the Court in **Newbury** noted, at paras [10] and [11], that there was no dispute that:

> "[10] ... even though the terms of paragraph 6 of Schedule 3 to CEMA appear to give the court in forfeiture proceedings no choice but to condemn the goods if they

> are 'liable to forfeiture' under the Act, the court must refuse to do this if to do so would be in breach of Mr Newbury's right's under the Community law: see **Conegate Ltd v HM Customs and Excise Commissioners** (case 121/85) [1987] QB 254."

and found that:

> "[35] … the issue of whether property is liable to forfeiture includes whether forfeiture would be so disproportionate as to be in breach of the particular claimant's rights under art 1 of the First Protocol to the convention and both can be resolved by the court. This is not strictly a question of discretion but a matter upon which the court is entitled to reach its own independent judgment.".

The decision in Newbury has been applied and followed in numerous cases involving condemnation proceedings involving vehicles seized under section 141(1)(a) CEMA and it is established that, e.g.:

> "… *Newbury*, it would appear, decides that condemnation is a discretionary remedy. I see no reason why consideration should not be given in proceedings of this kind, where the court accepts an importer's account that in substance and in fact the goods he brought in were for private use, whether an order of condemnation would not itself be disproportionate in the circumstances; if at any rate the importer undertakes to pay the duty." (**Stern v Director of Border Revenue** [2013] EWHC 553 (Admin) Laws LJ at para [15]).

Reliance is often placed in the course of condemnation proceedings on dicta from Lightman J in **Fox v Customs and Excise Commissioners** [2002] EWHC 1244 (Admin) who, when considering the effect of para 6 of Schedule 3 CEMA (in the context of Mr Fox's goods having been seized under section 141(1)(b) because they were "mixed, packed or found" with goods belonging to a Mr Fox's daughter's boyfriend, Mr Everett), stated:

> "[16] …the statutory language is mandatory: where the goods are liable to forfeiture the court is bound to condemn them. This is placed beyond question by the terms of paragraph 6 of Schedule 3 which expressly requires that the court 'shall' condemn as forfeited goods found liable to forfeiture at the date of seizure. …[Reference is made to **De Keyser v British Railway Traffic** [1936] 1 KB 224 and **Customs and Excise Commissioners v Air Canada** [1991] 2 QB 446] … The legislature in enacting the 1979 Act made plain its intention that the court should have no discretion and that there should be no doubt in the future on this question by the deliberate substitution in paragraph 6 of Schedule 3 of the word 'shall' for the word 'may' in the earlier Act.

However, that strict interpretation of para 6 of Schedule 3, particularly when dealing with primary (as opposed to secondary) forfeiture involving seizures of vehicles "constructed, adapted, altered or fitted in any manner for the purpose of concealing goods" under section 88 CEMA, should be viewed in the light of the remainder of Lightman J's judgment e.g.

> "[17] … Section 141(1)(b) upon its true construction only bites where the court finds as a fact in the proceedings relating to the seized goods that other goods are liable to forfeiture and that the seized goods are mixed, packed or found with those other goods. As a matter of common sense and as a matter of common justice it must be open to the owner of the seized goods, in this case Mr Fox, to

> challenge the facts relied on to establish the liability to forfeiture of the other party's, in this case Mr Evertt's, goods. It is nothing to the point that the other party, in this case Mr Everett, declines to make a claim or attend the hearing, and default decisions are accordingly mandated by the 1979 Act in respect of Mr Everett's goods. …
>
> [22] … Condemnation of Mr Fox's goods will only amount to a violation [of his rights under article 1 of the First Protocol] if it goes beyond what is proportionate in the circumstances of the particular case, including any findings of fact by the justices: see the **Air Canda** case …".

When considering the issue of proportionality, and bearing in mind the words of Stanley Burnton J in **Perinpanathan** (in the context of costs) that "it would not be sensible to try exhaustively to define such matters", the following factors may be relevant:

- the personal circumstances, including the finances, of the individual,
- the value of the goods (and the revenue evaded) and/or the vehicle involved,
- the conduct of the individual in the course of the interception and any subsequent correspondence and/or proceedings (e.g. a refusal to answer questions contrasted with a willingness to cooperate) and
- any previous dealings the individual has had with Border Force.

PART FOUR

RESTORATION PROCEEDINGS

CHAPTER TEN

RESTORATION

Statutory Framework

As stated above, the alternative means of challenging a seizure by means of condemnation proceedings is to request a review of the decision pursuant to section 152(b) CEMA which provides that:

> "the Commissioners may, as they see fit … (b) restore, subject to such conditions (if any) as they think proper, any thing forfeited or seized under [the customs and excise] Acts".

The Act provides a wide discretion to the Commissioners to impose conditions on any restoration (in contrast to the "all or nothing" options open to a court dealing with condemnation (**Newbury** at para [23]) but the reality is that strict policies are in place for any officer considering a review (e.g. **Gascoyne v Customs and Excise Commissioners** [2004] EWCA Civ 1162 where the policy to return vehicle used for smuggling only in exceptional cases was confirmed as reasonable).

The statutory provisions relating to reviews and appeal to the Tribunal are set out in sections 14 to 16 of the Finance Act 1994: in summary the relevant details are as follows:-

> A Notice requiring a review can be made by any person whose liability to pay any duty or penalty is affected by a decision under section 152(b), or to whom such a decision has been made, or to whom the conditions, restrictions, requirements, etc. of such a decision apply (section 14(2).

Such a Notice must be made (i.e. received by HMRC/Border Force – **BT Trasporti SRL in Liquidation v Director of Border Revenue** [2010] UKFTT 287 (TC)) in writing within 45 days of the original decision – section 14(3).

A review can be made out of time (section 14A(1)) where either HMRC are satisfied there was a reasonable excuse for not giving Notice within 45 days and the Notice was given without unreasonable delay thereafter or (if HMRC are not so satisfied) the Tribunal on request by the individual orders a review (section 14A(3) and (4). A Tribunal considering such a request will consider the purposes of the time limit, the length of and reason for the delay and the consequence of granting for refusing an extension of time (see **Data Select Limited v HMRC** [2012] UKUT 187, and **Leeds City Council v HMRC** [2014] UKUT 0350, but see also, e.g. **Tibor Mozer** [2021] UKFTT 475 (TC) where the overlap with the three stage test from **Denton v T H White Ltd** [2014] EWCA Civ 906) was considered.

The review decision must be given to the individual within 45 days of receipt of the Notice (failing which the original decision will be assumed to have been confirmed (section 15(2)(b)).

Any appeal to the Tribunal must be made within 30 days of the date of the review decision (section 16(1)) or, where there is an assumed confirmation pursuant to section 15(2)(b), 75 days of the Notice (section 16(1A)).

The powers of the Tribunal dealing with an appeal against a review decision

> "shall be confined to a power, where the tribunal are satisfied that the Commissioners or other person making that decision could not reasonably have arrived at it, to do one or more of the following
>
> (a) to direct that the decision, so far as it remains in force, is to cease to have effect from such time as the tribunal may direct;
>
> (b) to require the Commissioners to conduct, in accordance with the directions of the tribunal, a review or further review as appropriate of the original decision; and
>
> (c) in the case of a decision which has already been acted on or taken effect and cannot be remedied by a review or further review as appropriate, to declare the decision to have been unreasonable and to give directions to the Commissioners as to the steps to be taken for securing that repetitions of the unreasonableness do not occur when comparable circumstances arise in future." (section 16(4)).

In the ordinary course, the Tribunal having made a decision will provide its findings of fact and order the Commissioners to review the original review decision in the light of, and applying, those findings of fact. It is not unusual for a re-review to result in the same outcome as the original decision (e.g. a refusal to restore goods) which can lead to a further appeal. It is imperative that a re-review decision is read in conjunction with (and any further appeal is based on and makes reference to) the Tribunal's decision and, in particular, the facts found by the Tribunal.

The burden of proof lies on the appellant (i.e. the individual) "to show that the grounds on which any such appeal is brought have been established" (section 16(6)) so unlike condemnation proceedings, where it is for the Complainant to establish on the balance of probabilities that the goods, etc. are liable to forfeiture, in restoration proceedings "the boot is on the other foot".

CHAPTER ELEVEN

THE TRIBUNAL'S JURISDICTION

The Tribunal's jurisdiction is limited to determining whether the review decision was unreasonable, i.e. a decision that no reasonable person could have come to, applying the test derived from **Associated Provincial Picture Houses Ltd v Wednesbury Corporation** [1948] 1KB 223:

> "… the court is entitled to investigate the action of the local authority with a view to seeing whether it has taken into account matters which it ought not to take into account, or conversely, has refused to take into account or neglected to take into account matters which it ought to take into account. Once that question is answered in favour of the local authority, it may still be possible to say that the local authority, nevertheless, have come to a conclusion so unreasonable that no reasonable authority could ever have come to it. In such a case, again, I think the court can interfere. The power of the court to interfere in each case is not that of an appellate authority to override a decision of the local authority, but is that of a judicial authority which is concerned, and concerned only, to see whether the local authority have contravened the law by acting in excess of the powers which Parliament has confided in it." (Lord Greene MR at page 233)

or, in the context of the VAT Tribunal, in **John Dee v Customs and Excise Commissioners** [1995] STC 941, where Neill LJ refers to Lord

Lane's dicta in **Customs and Excise Commissioners v J H Corbitt (Numismatists) Ltd** [1981] AC 22 HL:

> "… the tribunal will, to adopt the language of Lord Lane, consider whether the commissioners have acted in a way in which no reasonable panel of commissioners could have acted or whether they had taken into account some irrelevant matter or had disregarded something to which they should have given weight. The tribunal may also have to consider whether the commissioners have erred on a point of law." (page 952g).

Significantly, the Tribunal does not have any jurisdiction to revisit the issue of whether the goods (or vehicle) were liable to forfeiture; that can only be determined in the course of condemnation proceedings (or pursuant to para 5 of Schedule 3) and the Tribunal does not permit the individual a "second bite of the cherry" or an alternative route of appeal against a condemnation decision/order (see **Gora v Customs and Excise Commissioners** [2003] EWCA Civ 525 and **Gascoyne v Customs and Excise Commissioners** [2003] EWHC 257 (Ch), affirmed by the Court of Appeal in [2004] EWCA Civ 1162).

The issue was considered further in **Revenue and Customs Commissioners v Jones** [2011] EWCA Civ 824 where Mr and Mrs Jones challenged the seizure of tobacco and alcohol and their car following a trip to Belgium, they gave notice of claim under para 3 of Schedule 3 but later withdrew that claim (resulting in a deemed condemnation under paragraph 5) and pursued a request for a review under section 152(b) CEMA. The First Tier Tribunal ("FTT") found that the goods had been imported for "personal use" pursuant to the pre-Brexit regime and so were not liable to forfeiture and should not have been condemned and the Upper Tribunal ("UT") confirmed that decision.

The matter proceeded to the Court of Appeal to determine whether the Tribunal had jurisdiction to determine whether the goods had been imported for personal use.

Mummery LJ considered the cases of **Gora** and **Gascoyne** and, at para [71] summarised the conclusions he had reached "for the future guidance of tribunals and their users", these included:

> "(1) The owners of goods seized by the customs officers could only be condemned as forfeit pursuant to an order of a court. The FTT and the UT are statutory appellate bodies that have not been given any such original jurisdiction. …
>
> (4) The stipulated statutory effect of the owners' withdrawal of their notice of claim … was that the goods were deemed by the express language of paragraph 5 to have been condemned *and* to have been 'duly' condemned as forfeited as illegally imported goods. The tribunal must give effect to the clear deeming provisions in the 1979 Act …
>
> (5) The deeming process limited the scope of the issues that the owners were entitled to ventilate in the FTT on their restoration appeal. The FTT had to take it that the goods had been 'duly' condemned as illegal imports. It was not open to it to conclude that the goods were legal imports illegally seized by HMRC by finding as a fact that they were being imported for personal use. The role of the tribunal, as defined by the 1979 Act, does not extend to deciding as a fact that the goods were, as the owners argued in the tribunal, being imported legally for personal use. That issue could only be decided by the court. The FTT's jurisdiction is limited to hearing an appeal against a

> discretionary decision by HMRC not to restore the seized goods to the owners.
>
> (9) … The Convention concerns [under Article 1 of the First Protocol and Article 6] expressed in Gascoyne are allayed once it has been appreciated, with the benefit of full argument on the 1979 Act, that there is no question of an owner of goods being deprived of them without having the legal right to have the lawfulness of seizure judicially determined one way or another by an impartial and independent court or tribunal: either through the courts on the issue of the legality of the seizure and/or through the FTT on the application of the principes of judicial review, such as reasonableness and proportionality, to the review decision of HMRC not to restore the goods to the owners."

The strict effect of Jones restricting the jurisdiction of the Tribunal led to some criticism of the decision which was firmly dealt with by Lewison LJ in **European Brand Trading Ltd v Commissioners of HM Revenue and Customs** [2016] EWCA Civ 90:

> "[41] Some tribunal judges have expressed dissatisfaction with HMRC v Jones. In reality, however, what they are dissatisfied with is the statutory scheme. But since this court has held in HMRC v Jones that the statutory procedure is Convention compliant, any perceived shortcomings in the scheme are matters for Parliament and not for the courts or tribunals. Their duty is to apply HMRC v Jones.".

The statutory limitation on the Tribunal's powers is also relevant to the issue of compensation where goods have been destroyed and compensation is payable in lieu of their return; it is open to the individual to challenge the level of compensation offered by Border Force and, if they do not agree the sum, to appeal that decision to the Tribunal (see **Powell** [2005] Lexis Citation 3995). The Tribunal, however, cannot impose its own assessment of the compensation payable but must simply send the matter back for a further review by Border Force.

CHAPTER TWELVE

PROPORTIONALITY

As indicated in **Jones**, the Tribunal's jurisdiction includes consideration of the issue of the proportionality of the effect of the decision in the particular situation.

The question of proportionality was previously considered in **Lindsay v Customs and Excise Commissioners** [2002] EWCA Civ 267 in the context of the Commissioners' policy of refusing to return vehicles seized (under section 141(1)(a) CEMA) which was that:

> "8.... any car or light goods vehicle (other than rented) used for smuggling or for transporting smuggled or diverted excise goods within the UK will be seized and not restored. Restoration will be very much the exception, not the rule, irrespective of whether it is the first time the smuggler has been caught. This policy is to be applied vigorously both at the *ports and at all inland locations* where it can be proved that a vehicle was used to transport goods which are liable to seizure ...
>
> 11. ... in general, the decision to restore should be because: it would be entirely disproportionate to refuse to restore the vehicle (one example could be on a first time 'technical' offence where a minimal amount of tobacco has been [brought] back for a relative's consumption with payment at costs); it would be seen as inhumane not to restore" (Lord Phillips MR at para 21).

Lord Phillips MR went on to confirm that:

"52 The commissioners' policy involves the deprivation of people's possessions. Under article 1 of the First Protocol to the Convention such deprivations will only be justified if it is in the public interest. More specifically, the deprivation can be justified if it is 'to secure the payment of taxes or other contributions or penalties'. The action taken must, however, strike a fair balance between the rights of the individual and the public interest. There must be a reasonable relationship of proportionality between the means employed and the aim pursued … one must consider the individual's case to ensure that the penalty imposed is fair. However strong the public interest, it cannot justify subjecting an individual to an interference with his fundamental rights that is unconscionable.

55. Broadly speaking, the aim of the commissioners' policy is the prevention of the evasion of excise duty that is imposed in accordance with European Community law. That is a legitimate aim under article 1 of the First Protocol to the Convention. The issue is whether the policy is liable to result in a penalty in the individual case that is disproportionate having regard to that particular aim.

63 … Those who deliberately use their vehicle to further fraudulent commercial ventures in the knowledge that if they are caught their cars will be rendered liable to forfeiture cannot reasonably be heard to complain if they lose those vehicles. Nor does it seems to me that, in such circumstances, the value of the car used need be taken into consideration. Those circumstances will normally take the case beyond the threshold where that factor can carry significant weight in the balance. Cases of exceptional

> hardship must always, of course be given due consideration.
>
> 64. The commissioners' policy does not, however, draw a distinction between the commercial smuggler and the driver importing goods for social distribution to family of friends in circumstances where there is no attempt to make a profit. Of course, even in such a case the scale of the importation, or other circumstances, may be such as to justify forfeiture of the car. Butt where the importation is not for the purpose of making a profit, I consider that the principle of proportionality requires that each case should be considered on its particular facts, which will include the scale of importation, whether it is a 'first offence', whether there was an attempt at concealment or dissimulation, the value of the vehicle and the degree of hardship that will be caused by forfeiture. There is open to the commissioners a wide range of lesser sanctions that will enable them to impose a sanction that is proportionate where forfeiture of the vehicle is not justified."

Lord Phillips MR's summary of the test to be applied (at para 52, above) was considered by the Supreme Court in **J P Whitter (Water Well Engineers) Ltd v Revenue and Customs Commissioners** [2018] UKSC 31, dealing with HMRC's decision to remove a registration under the Construction Industry Scheme (providing an advantageous trading status) which would have a significant adverse effect on the firm; it was held that any interference was proportionate given the tightly drawn parameters of, and the importance of securing compliance with, the Scheme.

In **Lindsay** the Tribunal decision under appeal had been that, contrary to the Reviewing Officer's decision, the vehicle should be restored and the commissioners should pay Mr Lindsay compensation for the loss of his "beautiful new ... Millenium Special Edition of a Ford Focus, coloured yellow" (para 1).

Lord Phillips MR found that:

> "69 … The tribunal have done more than direct that Review Officer Florence's decision ceased to have effect. They have purported to reverse it. That is something they had no jurisdiction to do."

and ordered that the Commissioners conduct a further review reflecting the Tribunal's decision and Court of Appeal's judgment.

While the criteria identified in Lindsay remain relevant to any proportionality argument, the removal of the "personal use" provisions and the application of the personal allowances inevitably impacts on the assessment of the "scale of the importation" in comparison to the other factors.

CHAPTER THIRTEEN

PROCEDURE ON APPEAL TO THE FIRST TIER TRIBUNAL TAX CHAMBER

The Tribunal Procedure (First-Tier Tribunal) (Tax Chamber) Rules 2009 (S.I. 2009 No 273) set out the procedure to be followed by the Tribunal in detail but a brief overview may be of assistance.

The Tribunal operates subject to the "overriding objective" i.e. to deal with cases fairly and justly which include "avoiding unnecessary formality and seeking flexibility in the proceedings" (Rule 2(2)(b)) and seeking to bring to the parties attention and "if the parties wish ... to facilitate the use of [any appropriate alternative] procedure for the resolution of the dispute" (Rule 3(1)(a) and (b)).

The Tribunal has a wide discretion to regulate its own procedure (Rule 5(1) and (3)(a) to (l)) and to make directions e.g. as regards the issues on which it requires evidence or submissions and the nature and means of providing such evidence or submissions, including the preparation of bundles (Rule 15).

Parties may apply for directions either in writing or orally during the course of a hearing (Rule 6(2)); such an application "must include the reasons for making that application" (Rule 6(3) and can be challenged by a further application (Rule 6(5)). Any direction must be complied with by 5 pm on the day appointed, or the next working day if the appointed day is a weekend or bank holiday (Rule 12).

The Tribunal has power to strike out a party's case in the event of non-compliance with directions or if "the Tribunal considers there is no reasonable prospect of the appellant's case, or part of it, succeeding" (Rule 8(3)). **Revenue and Customs Commissioners v BPP Holdings Ltd** [2016] EWCA Civ 121 confirmed that a strict approach should be taken when dealing with issues of non-compliance and striking out of cases or barring parties from proceedings and the reasons for non-compliance and any prejudice to the parties should be considered

The usual situation is that each side will bear their own costs but the Tribunal may make an order for costs if (a party or their representative has acted unreasonably in bringing, defending or conducting the proceedings" (Rule 10(1(b)), but the Tribunal "may not make an order … without first (a) giving that person an opportunity to make representations; and (b) if the paying person is an individual, considering that person's financial means." (Rule 10(5)); see also Chapter 14, **Costs in Restoration Proceedings**, below

A party may appoint a representative (who does not have to be a "legal representative" i.e. a solicitor or barrister), subject to the provision of a written notice confirming the appointment to the Tribunal and any other party to the proceedings (Rule 11).

Rule 15(2) provides that

> "The Tribunal may
>
> (a) admit evidence whether or not the evidence would be admissible in a civil trial in the United Kingdom; or
>
> (b) exclude evidence that would otherwise be admissible where-
>
>> (i) the evidence was not provided within the time allowed by a direction or practice direction;

(ii) the evidence was otherwise provided in a manner that did not comply with a direction or a practice direction; or

(iii) it would be otherwise unfair to admit the evidence.".

The Tribunal can make orders prohibiting the disclosure or publication of particular documents or the identification of any person (Rule 14) and has the power to compel the attendance of witnesses or the production of documents in the possession of any person (Rule 16).

A party may withdraw their claim either in writing or orally at a hearing and then has 28 days to seek its reinstatement (Rule 17).

Where different cases "give rise to common or related issues of fact or law" the Tribunal may appoint one as a lead case and stay the other(s) (Rule 18).

Rule 20 details the requirements for starting an appeal (i.e. against a review decision) before the Tribunal and the standard form "T240 Notice of Appeal" can either be completed online or a paper version can be used.

The notice of appeal must provide the name and address of the appellant and their representative (if any), a contact address for service of documents, details of the decision being appealed (including a written record of the decision and any written reasons), the result being sought and the grounds for the appeal (Rule 20). The Notice of Appeal should be sent to the Tribunal who will then notify the Respondent.

The Tribunal operates a system for allocating appeals as:

- Default Papers cases (which can be dealt with on paper i.e. without a hearing),
- Basic Cases (involving relatively little disclosure of evidence or statements prior to the hearing),
- Standard Cases (requiring more detailed case management) and
- Complex Cases (Rule 23).

Restoration appeals tend to fall into the Basic or Standard categories.

The Respondent must then provide a Statement of Case to the Tribunal and the other parties within 42 days (in a Default case) or 60 days (in a Standard or Complex Case) (Rule 25(1)). The Respondent can ask for an extension of time but the Statement of Case should specifically request the extension and the reason why it was not provided in time (Rule 25(4)).

In Default cases the Appellant has 30 days from the date of the Respondent's Statement of Case (not the date the Appellant received it) to provide the Tribunal and any other party with a Reply giving their response to the Statement of Case, any further information to be relied upon and requesting a hearing (Rule 26). If any party has, in writing, requested a hearing the Tribunal must hold a hearing (Rule 26(7)).

In Standard and Complex cases all parties must, within 42 days of the date of the Respondent's Statement of Case, provide each other with a list of (relevant) documents which they possess, have the right to possess or the right to take copies of and which they intend to rely upon in the proceedings and "must allow each other party to inspect or take copies of the documents on the list (except any documents which are privileged)" (Rule 27).

The Tribunal must hold a hearing (save for certain specified situations) before making a decision save when all parties have consented to such a course and the Tribunal considers it can decide the matter without a hearing (Rule 29) and the parties are entitled to attend the hearing (Rule 30) and to be given "reasonable notice of the time and place of any hearing" (Rule 31(1)) which, in the cases of a disposal hearing, must be at least 14 days, save with the parties consent or in urgent or exceptional circumstances (Rule 31(2)). The hearing will usually be in public (Rule 32).

"Batting Order" at the Hearing

Given that the proceedings are civil and the burden of proof lies on the appellant (i.e. the individual) they (or their representative) will have the opportunity to address the Tribunal to open their case (although this is frequently dispensed with or replaced with a "housekeeping discussion" where the issue are identified/confirmed and the logistics of the hearing are determined). They will then be expected to call their evidence, adopting any witness statement and being examined in chief (if permitted by the Tribunal), be cross-examined by the other side and asked any questions in re-examination by their representative and by the Tribunal. The Respondent will then call their evidence in similar fashion and then the parties (Respondent then Appellant) will make their closing submissions.

This is, of course, subject to the rules (above) providing for flexibility, allowing the Tribunal to manage its own procedure and to act proportionately, justly and fairly.

Decisions

Decisions may be announced orally at the end of a hearing but a written decision must be provided which states the decision and either (i) a summary of the findings of fact and reasons for the decision or (ii) full written findings of fact and reasons for the decision and notifies the parties of their right of appeal, unless otherwise agreed by the parties (Rule 35). The rules indicate that the decision should be given "within 28 days … or as soon as practicable thereafter" (Rule 35(2)).

The Rules also provide for correcting any "clerical mistake or other accidental slips or omission in a decision, direction or any document" (i.e. "the slip rule") (Rule 37) and the setting aside of a decision where it is in the interests of justice and (i) documents were not sent or received in time, (ii) there has been a procedural irregularity or (iii) a party (or their representative) was not present at a hearing (Rule 38).

Any application for permission to appeal a Tribunal decision must be made (received by the Tribunal) in writing within 56 days of the decision, unless it includes a request for an extension of time for appealing with the reasons why it was not made in time and the Tribunal extends time pursuant to Rule 5(3)(a), and must identify the decision subject to the appeal, the alleged error(s) in the decision and the result sought by the person making the application (Rule (39)).

The Tribunal must then consider whether to review the decision "if it is satisfied that there was an error of law in the decision" (Rule 41((1)(b)) and, if it "decides not to review the decision, or reviews the decision and decides to take no action in relation to the decision, or a part of it the Tribunal must consider whether to give permission to appeal in relation to the decision or that part of it" (Rule 40(2)) and "send a record of its decision to the parties as soon as practicable" and, if it refuses permission, must send a statement of its reasons for refusal and notify the party of its right to apply to the Upper Tribunal for permission to appeal (Rule 40(3) and (4)).

CHAPTER FOURTEEN

COSTS IN RESTORATION PROCEEDINGS

As indicated above, the usual, default position in Tribunal proceedings is for each party to bear their own costs regardless of the outcome, however Rule 10 provides for costs where a party has behaved unreasonably; this issue arises most frequently in cases where it is suggested (or found) that a party's case is unmeritorious and should not have been pursued or where a party withdraws late from proceedings.

Distinctive Care Ltd v Revenue and Customs Commissioners [2019] EWCA Civ 1010 is the leading case on the issue of costs in the Tribunal and was helpfully considered in **Lenity Ltd v Commissioners of Customs and Excise** [2021] UKFTT 0272 (TC) which summarised the relevant principles as follows:

> "16. The leading and binding authority on the question of unreasonable costs is Distinctive Care Ltd v HMRC … In that case, and by reference to the approval of the Upper Tribunal judgment, it was determined:
>
> > (1) The earliest conduct that was relevant in the context of determining whether a party had behaved unreasonably was the point at which the proceedings commenced with the issue of a notice of appeal as the discretion applies only to

unreasonable conduct in the proceedings and not to the investigation leading to those proceedings.

(2) The focus of the Tribunal was to be the handling of the litigation and not as to the quality of the original decision. The Tribunal is warned that the award of costs should not represent a wide-ranging analysis of the parties' conduct prior to the appeal.

(3) The granting of an unreasonable costs order is not to be seen as a 'back-door' means of costs shifting with the consequence that what constitutes unreasonable behaviour is unlikely to extend to improper or negligent behaviour.

(4) Where a party withdraws from an appeal it is necessary to consider whether they had acted promptly once it was identified that the proceedings were to be discontinued.

(5) Where costs are awarded on the grounds of unreasonable behaviour the scope of the costs award may include costs incurred prior to the commencement of proceedings provided that such costs are within the scope of the ultimate appeal.

17. In respect of the approach to be taken to considering whether a decision to withdraw amounts to unreasonable conduct the Tribunal is also bound to follow the approach directed by the Upper Tribunal in **Tarafdur v HMRC** [2014] UKUT 00362 in which the Upper Tribunal considered the approach to be to answer the following questions:

> (1) What was the reason for withdrawal of that party from the appeal?
>
> (2) Having regard to that reason, could that party have withdrawn at an earlier stage in proceedings?
>
> (3) Was it unreasonable for that party to not to have withdrawn at an earlier stage?".

When determining what constitutes unreasonable behaviour in **Leslie Wallis** [2013] UKFTT 81 (TC) the Tribunal said that:

> "27. It seems to us that it cannot be that any wrong assertion by a party to an appeal is automatically unreasonable ... The rules clearly do not intend that just because a party is wrong that that party should be ordered to pay the other's costs ... In our judgment before making a wrong assertion constitutes unreasonable conduct in an appeal that party must generally persist in it in the face of unbeatable argument that he is wrong. Thus for example a party who persists in a legal argument which is precisely the same as one recently dismissed in the Supreme Court and which has been drawn to his attention ... could be acting unreasonably...".

In **Barrell Booze t/a Cellarvino** [2015] UKFTT 347 (TC) the Tribunal referred to **Wallis** and confirmed that:

> "27. ... the party would not be acting unreasonably when pursuing a case without merit unless he ought to have known his case was without merit...".

MORE BOOKS BY LAW BRIEF PUBLISHING

A selection of our other titles available now:-

'A Practical Guide to the Independent School Standards – September 2023 Edition' by Sarah McKimm
'A Practical Guide to Estate Administration and Crypto Assets' by Richard Marshall
'A Practical Guide to Managing GDPR Data Subject Access Requests – Second Edition' by Patrick O'Kane
'A Practical Guide to Parental Alienation in Private and Public Law Children Cases' by Sam King QC & Frankie Shama
'Contested Heritage – Removing Art from Land and Historic Buildings' by Richard Harwood QC, Catherine Dobson, David Sawtell
'The Limits of Separate Legal Personality: When Those Running a Company Can Be Held Personally Liable for Losses Caused to Third Parties Outside of the Company' by Dr Mike Wilkinson
'A Practical Guide to Transgender Law' by Robin Moira White & Nicola Newbegin
'A Practical Guide to 'Stranded Spouses' in Family Law' by Mani Singh Basi
'A Practical Guide to Residential Freehold Conveyancing' by Lorraine Richardson
'A Practical Guide to Pensions on Divorce for Lawyers' by Bryan Scant
'A Practical Guide to Challenging Sham Marriage Allegations in Immigration Law' by Priya Solanki
'A Practical Guide to Digital Communications Evidence in Criminal Law' by Sam Willis
'A Practical Guide to Legal Rights in Scotland' by Sarah-Jane Macdonald
'A Practical Guide to New Build Conveyancing' by Paul Sams & Rebecca East
'A Practical Guide to Defending Barristers in Disciplinary Cases' by Marc Beaumont
'A Practical Guide to Inherited Wealth on Divorce' by Hayley Trim
'A Practical Guide to Practice Direction 12J and Domestic Abuse in Private Law Children Proceedings' by Rebecca Cross & Malvika Jaganmohan

'A Practical Guide to Confiscation and Restraint' by Narita Bahra QC, John Carl Townsend, David Winch
'A Practical Guide to the Law of Forests in Scotland' by Philip Buchan
'A Practical Guide to Health and Medical Cases in Immigration Law' by Rebecca Chapman & Miranda Butler
'A Practical Guide to Bad Character Evidence for Criminal Practitioners by Aparna Rao
'A Practical Guide to Extradition Law post-Brexit' by Myles Grandison et al
'A Practical Guide to Hoarding and Mental Health for Housing Lawyers' by Rachel Coyle
'A Practical Guide to Psychiatric Claims in Personal Injury – 2nd Edition' by Liam Ryan
'Stephens on Contractual Indemnities' by Richard Stephens
'A Practical Guide to the EU Succession Regulation' by Richard Frimston
'A Practical Guide to Solicitor and Client Costs – 2nd Edition' by Robin Dunne
'Constructive Dismissal – Practice Pointers and Principles' by Benjimin Burgher
'A Practical Guide to Religion and Belief Discrimination Claims in the Workplace' by Kashif Ali
'A Practical Guide to the Law of Medical Treatment Decisions' by Ben Troke
'Fundamental Dishonesty and QOCS in Personal Injury Proceedings: Law and Practice' by Jake Rowley
'A Practical Guide to the Law in Relation to School Exclusions' by Charlotte Hadfield & Alice de Coverley
'A Practical Guide to Divorce for the Silver Separators' by Karin Walker
'The Right to be Forgotten – The Law and Practical Issues' by Melissa Stock
'A Practical Guide to Planning Law and Rights of Way in National Parks, the Broads and AONBs' by James Maurici QC, James Neill et al
'A Practical Guide to Election Law' by Tom Tabori
'A Practical Guide to the Law in Relation to Surrogacy' by Andrew Powell
'A Practical Guide to Claims Arising from Fatal Accidents – 2nd Edition' by James Patience
'A Practical Guide to the Ownership of Employee Inventions – From Entitlement to Compensation' by James Tumbridge & Ashley Roughton
'A Practical Guide to Asbestos Claims' by Jonathan Owen & Gareth McAloon

'A Practical Guide to Stamp Duty Land Tax in England and Northern Ireland' by Suzanne O'Hara
'A Practical Guide to the Law of Farming Partnerships' by Philip Whitcomb
'Covid-19, Homeworking and the Law – The Essential Guide to Employment and GDPR Issues' by Forbes Solicitors
'Covid-19 and Criminal Law – The Essential Guide' by Ramya Nagesh
'Covid-19 and Family Law in England and Wales – The Essential Guide' by Safda Mahmood
'A Practical Guide to the Law of Unlawful Eviction and Harassment – 2nd Edition' by Stephanie Lovegrove
'Covid-19, Brexit and the Law of Commercial Leases – The Essential Guide' by Mark Shelton
'A Practical Guide to Costs in Personal Injury Claims – 2nd Edition' by Matthew Hoe
'A Practical Guide to the General Data Protection Regulation (GDPR) – 2nd Edition' by Keith Markham
'Ellis on Credit Hire – Sixth Edition' by Aidan Ellis & Tim Kevan
'A Practical Guide to Working with Litigants in Person and McKenzie Friends in Family Cases' by Stuart Barlow
'Protecting Unregistered Brands: A Practical Guide to the Law of Passing Off' by Lorna Brazell
'A Practical Guide to Secondary Liability and Joint Enterprise Post-Jogee' by Joanne Cecil & James Mehigan
'A Practical Guide to the Pre-Action RTA Claims Protocol for Personal Injury Lawyers' by Antonia Ford
'A Practical Guide to Neighbour Disputes and the Law' by Alexander Walsh
'A Practical Guide to Forfeiture of Leases' by Mark Shelton
'A Practical Guide to Coercive Control for Legal Practitioners and Victims' by Rachel Horman
'A Practical Guide to the Law of Driverless Cars – Second Edition' by Alex Glassbrook, Emma Northey & Scarlett Milligan
'A Practical Guide to TOLATA Claims' by Greg Williams
'A Practical Guide to Elderly Law – 2nd Edition' by Justin Patten
'A Practical Guide to Responding to Housing Disrepair and Unfitness Claims' by Iain Wightwick

'A Practical Guide to the Law of Bullying and Harassment in the Workplace' by Philip Hyland
'How to Be a Freelance Solicitor: A Practical Guide to the SRA-Regulated Freelance Solicitor Model' by Paul Bennett
'A Practical Guide to Prison Injury Claims' by Malcolm Johnson
'A Practical Guide to the Small Claims Track – 2nd Edition' by Dominic Bright
'A Practical Guide to Advising Clients at the Police Station' by Colin Stephen McKeown-Beaumont
'A Practical Guide to Antisocial Behaviour Injunctions' by Iain Wightwick
'Practical Mediation: A Guide for Mediators, Advocates, Advisers, Lawyers, and Students in Civil, Commercial, Business, Property, Workplace, and Employment Cases' by Jonathan Dingle with John Sephton
'The Mini-Pupillage Workbook' by David Boyle
'A Practical Guide to Crofting Law' by Brian Inkster
'A Practical Guide to the Law of Domain Names and Cybersquatting' by Andrew Clemson
'A Practical Guide to the Law of Gender Pay Gap Reporting' by Harini Iyengar
'NHS Whistleblowing and the Law' by Joseph England
'Employment Law and the Gig Economy' by Nigel Mackay & Annie Powell
'A Practical Guide to Noise Induced Hearing Loss (NIHL) Claims' by Andrew Mckie, Ian Skeate, Gareth McAloon
'An Introduction to Beauty Negligence Claims – A Practical Guide for the Personal Injury Practitioner' by Greg Almond
'Intercompany Agreements for Transfer Pricing Compliance' by Paul Sutton
'Zen and the Art of Mediation' by Martin Plowman
'A Practical Guide to the SRA Principles, Individual and Law Firm Codes of Conduct 2019 – What Every Law Firm Needs to Know' by Paul Bennett
'A Practical Guide to Adoption for Family Lawyers' by Graham Pegg
'A Practical Guide to Industrial Disease Claims' by Andrew Mckie & Ian Skeate
'A Practical Guide to Conducting a Sheriff Court Proof' by Andrew Stevenson
'A Practical Guide to Vicarious Liability' by Mariel Irvine
'A Practical Guide to Applications for Landlord's Consent and Variation of Leases' by Mark Shelton
'A Practical Guide to Relief from Sanctions Post-Mitchell and Denton' by Peter Causton

www.ingramcontent.com/pod-product-compliance
Lightning Source LLC
LaVergne TN
LVHW022101200926
848481LV00003B/1025
9781916698390